LIVING WITH CEREBRAL PALSY

A COLLECTION OF INSPIRING STORIES FROM

CP WARRIORS WORLDWIDE

Created by

KYLE N. SCOTT

Kyle N. Scott

Published by The Book Chief Publishing House 2023

Suite 2A, Blackthorn House, St Paul's Square, Birmingham, B3 1RL

www.thebookchief.com

ISBN No: 978-1-7388734-0-1

Book Cover Design: Deearo Marketing
Editing / Proofreading: Sharon Brown
Typesetting: Sharon Brown
/ Publishing: Sharon Brown

THE BOOK CHIEF®

IGNITE YOUR WRITING

Table of Contents

Foreword

By Elizabeth Pietrantonio

Writer and Former Associate Dean

I first met Kyle when he appeared in my Drafting and CAD lab. I had two students that year who were in wheelchairs, so I was already prepared with drafting boards that lowered to wheelchair height and extra space between the aisles. But Kyle was different. I could see right away that Kyle could not hold a drafting pencil. Now, I thought, this is going to be a challenge!

After finishing the first lecture, I walked around the lab, making sure students were clear about the first assignment – construction lines, straight lettering, and rolling pencils slowly while making a line.

Then I came to Kyle. I liked him right away! He wasn't anxious and wasn't even concerned that there was no drafting pencil in sight. He looked at me with a great big grin, which I always see on his face – and waited for me to think through his options. He already knew what he couldn't do and had confidence that together, we would come up with a plan for what he could do. And we did.

The best part of Kyle is his optimism. Since that first encounter years ago, I have been watching his journey on the sidelines.

He brings enthusiasm, optimism and complete engagement to every project he tackles – big or small. I continue, even now, opening e-mails from Kyle with a smile on my face wondering what he is into now and how exciting it is likely to be.

When Kyle first started writing, I was also starting but slightly ahead of him. He questioned me about everything, and before I knew it, he had taken off! He has a great view of the world from that chair. He is a master in the use of social media, and he has built a support team around himself that rivals anything I have ever seen. In a book I read a long while ago, The Tipping Point by Malcolm Gladwell, the author talks about connecting with people and how important it is to develop a good network. Kyle should be one of his case studies!

Kyle's writing has touched a lot of people. He is open, and he is honest. When we meet, I always assume he can do anything. And if he can't, he tells me straight up. He has taught me a lot about living with Cerebral Palsy, but it is interesting to read reviews of his writing and to read the word 'disability' in those reviews. I never think of Kyle as having a disability – I think of Kyle's way of life. Of course, it is different from mine, but he meets challenges much better than I do. And he takes on any new direction with an abandonment and joy that makes everyone he meets feel the same way too.

Introduction

As part of my journey to becoming an inspiring author of my memoir, In A Split Second: Living with Cerebral Palsy, I came across a publishing and media company called MO2VATE Media which incorporates The Book Chief Publishing House, located in Birmingham, England. This platform provides credible authority across industries for growth-driven business owners through writing, speaking, and publishing opportunities.

It has been a privilege to join the MO2VATE Media community, where I have shared various stories with the hope that they would inspire, educate and help others, giving hope to the next generations with disabilities and those struggling with life in general. You should never feel ashamed of sharing your story; it might just be what someone out there needs to hear to feel less alone.

Sharon Brown, the Founder of MO2VATE Media, opened many unexpected doors. I am honoured to have my article "The Unseen Struggles of Cerebral Palsy" named as one of the finalists in the Best Overall and Most Inspirational categories of the 2021 International MO2VATE Awards.

In 2022, I won the Editor's Choice Award for my raw and emotional article "Disadvantaged Man." In 2022, Sharon created an opportunity to contribute to a collaborative book for ten inspiring men, including myself, from around the world which allowed us to share our adversity-to-triumph stories.

After participating in the collaboration book, I was inspired to gather people with Cerebral Palsy from around the world to share their hopes, dreams, challenges, obstacles, rejections, triumphs and how we continue to live life to the fullest.

I believe everyone has an inspirational story to share if only they were brave enough to do so. Do not let your restrictions or critics dictate what you can or cannot do. You can overcome even the toughest physical challenges if you look hard and work with the right people. Never give up and keep going no matter what. Take each challenge as an opportunity to grow, and flip your stories to the outcome you've always wanted. It is your movie, and you are the star, so be brave enough to act out your "desires chapter."

THIS IS YOUR LIFE!

Thank you, Sharon, for allowing me to achieve a dream I would never have imagined possible.

My co-authors and I would like to thank our readers for purchasing this book.

Dedication

To Mark E. Smith . . . a young man who had Cerebral Palsy. My life is made more meaningful by his memoir, which gave me the courage and strength to challenge myself; to find my happiness in life.

Everyone from family, friends, EA's, teachers, coaches, teammates and all the others I have met along the way who have welcomed me with open arms and love. You have also given me hope and faith.

I am privileged and thankful for everyone who has been a part of my journey.

CHAPTER 1

LIVING WITH CEREBRAL PALSY

By Amanda Fino

Virginia, USA

www.youtube.com/@cpgalsworld / https://linktr.ee/cpgalsworld

Cerebral Palsy can be complicated and sometimes painful, both mentally and physically. However, in addition to cerebral palsy, the doctor diagnosed me with Complex Post-Traumatic stress disorder and other mental health issues.

Yet, I learned that I'm not alone. It's WE, not I, in the fight for a cure for CP. I can feel it in my bones that we are so close to a treatment — not just for CP but for all disabilities if we stop wasting money on things.

I love waking up each morning to the sweet smell of coffee and going downstairs to a fresh cup waiting for me, along with my morning greeting from my dad. While the 6am start of Fox and Friends appears on TV, we go back and forth between CNN and MSNBC News.

For about an hour, dad and I discuss anything new that is going on in our lives. I never saw myself being a thirty-something-year-old drinking coffee, watching the news, and being grateful for each new day.

After coffee, I take the six-morning pills that help me deal with my cerebral palsy and mental health.

Then I head upstairs, turn on my computer to what I call the Facebook world, and start the day while having a cup of coffee with my beloved friend Heaven, as we talk about everything.

I live in Williamsburg, VA. As an author, along with my friend Cyndi Anderson, I am writing a Christian autobiography about my life with cerebral palsy entitled CP Gal's World, Flying with My Disability. As well as speaking to people with disabilities, I am working on becoming a Christian disability speaker.

I am here today as a self-advocate, a proud Virginian, a concerned citizen, and a member of the Training Alumni Association (T.A.A.). An association of the Partners in Policymaking program graduates and the Youth Leadership Academy supported by the Virginia Board for People with Disabilities facilitates grassroots advocacy. I'm a proud graduate of the class of 2020.

I was born with cerebral Palsy as a result of a difficult birth. However, I have decided to wear my CP as a badge of courage. I'm ready to talk about my traumatic childhood, including physical, mental, sexual, and emotional abuse.

While coping with my father's death from cancer at age fifty-nine, my biological mother changed from a loving mother to someone who hated me. This resulted in her having me locked up through my teen years in my own family home.

My mom led me to believe that anger and hate were the way to live. I've survived three murder attempts by her hand. I felt like an animal, a monster that needed to be locked up. My mom tried to get me locked up in a mental asylum or a group home for disabled people so she could forget about me — acting like I was never her daughter.

Life itself drove me to the near edge on several occasions. It was a chance meeting with a former U.S. intelligence officer, his Russian-born wife, and their son that saved my life. They opened up their home — giving me a chance to be part of a loving family I had so dearly craved. We are in the adoption process, and I'm adding their family name, Fino, to my last name.

With all of life's curves, twists, turns, and crossroads. With all the road construction and getting lost, it was a miracle that I arrived home at last: 26 years, nine months, and 22 days later!

The A.D.A. was passed into law 110 days after I was born. I have the right to fly on an aeroplane alone. I have the right to go to school and study with an I.E.P. getting my O.T., P.T., and speech therapy for me.

I have hundreds of ideas for improvement. Income is often a barrier to attending social events and being visible. We should have discounts, like the military and the elderly have. Why do we look at people with disabilities like we do today, I ask you? Things are better, but sometimes the world forgets about people with disabilities giving us lip service. In the early 1900s, people with disabilities were sent off to state institutions or, even worse, to jail. I was heartbroken and disturbed when I read about what took place in the book, "Christmas in Purgatory" (1965). It was by far the most unearthly thing that Americans ever did.

In 2015, I remember touring a facility for disabled adults in another state. It was located in a dangerous, depressed neighborhood. There were bars on the windows to keep them in and the neighbors out. At twenty-five years of age, I felt like the staff treated disabled adults like cattle. When I looked at the people who were there, they were miserable.

The rooms were not temperature-controlled and were dilapidated. I was angry with the authorities, the uncaring community, and the disrespect. I was in tears.

My dream for the future is to help open what I call luxury disability living. Gloving is required by law to prevent the spread of disease among staff and patients. However, it also leads to distancing the team from the residents. I want to make room decor inviting, allow food choices at meals, encourage outside guests at meals, and provide space for community meetings. Why do we have to wait until we are 65 years old to experience senior living at its best?

Providing shopping and cultural expeditions also makes us visible to the public. Regular access to transportation would allow people with disabilities to access the community just like anyone else. People could complete their shopping, try an adventurous new experience, or even go to the spa. Should people with disabilities be able to go to a resort if they want to? Heck, yes! Why not enjoy life like others?

I'm going to just put it like it is. In my view, I am not a hero or that gal that you call "inspiring." I have blown it and messed things up, including many relationships in the past. God is magnificent and has helped me become a better person today. Before, I had a horrible temper; I was not the kind of person you would want to know.

I am not scared to talk about my long list of mistakes and sins. I wish I could change the past, but I don't have my magic wand to redo history. I thank God daily for his power to heal and allow me to become CP Gal.

I'm trying my best to become one of the voices of those who, through disability, cannot speak for themselves.

I'm not out for myself; I'm out for that friend who went into an institution for life because of her CP. And that friend who can't talk or walk uses a wheelchair and his iPad to communicate.

I am here to fight for disability rights, not for personal gain. I want to help change the whole world's point of view on how they view a person with a disability being out in public. I recall once, on a shopping trip, I tried on a very sexy dress; I showed it to my mother. There were two ladies in the dressing room, and one of them said:

"If I had her body, I would wear that dress, but she can't." I was very hurt by what was said.

Another time, a female doctor refused to give me a Pap smear due to my CP just because sex would be hard for me to comprehend. I am sorry to tell you that my biggest pet peeves are pity, lip service, and being treated like a baby.

Here's my point of view: We all have the same color of blood, we are all equal, so we should all be treated the same . . . To me, that is God's number one rule. Please don't pity me. Why would you? I'm just like you. Don't get me wrong, on several occasions, I was driven to the near edge of life until I opened the Bible to read God's word and meet my savior Jesus Christ.

During our conversations, I discussed my desire to find a good neighborhood church with my recently connected Godmother, Liz. Also, I've talked about finding a church with Dad for a while.

Using Google to search "church near me," I discovered a Presbyterian (PCA) Church with values similar to mine that seemed like they fit. Note: my Godma's pastor texted her back that moment, saying it was the only church he would have recommended in Williamsburg! Lucky me, it wasn't across town.

On Aug 8, 2021, my dad and I visited this Presbyterian Church after introducing myself via email and explaining myself and my CP. Moments after stepping into its open window chapel, I knew I had found what I was looking for in my lifetime, welcome home Amanda. As if this was waiting for me to find, I was at peace and peace with God. It was a place I could see myself growing in, growing older, and taking this church as my second home.

Within a few weeks, I seemed to like this church more. I met my beloved sister and Bible teacher Cyndi, her husband and her mom.

As a result, I joined their six-week discovery course. I just had to decide whether or not this church was the right one for me. I joined the church, upholding my vows and showing my commitment. Getting baptized at my new church was especially important since I was never baptized as a child.

On a cold chilly day on Nov 21, 2021, in the name of the Father, Son, and Holy Spirit, I was baptized at age thirty-one in front of family and friends in my church, either live or via live streaming.

During my baptism, everyone watching was moved as if the Holy Spirit came upon us and gave me a new heart. As stated in the Bible, "*I will give you a new heart and put a new spirit within you; I will take the heart of stone out of your flesh and give you a heart of flesh." (Ezekiel 36:26 NKJV)* God indeed put into me a new heart along with a new set of eyes like Paul on the road to Damascus.

That was one of the most important days of my life. Since then, I have fully embraced being part of my church while making new friends. The Christmas eve church candlelight service is particularly enjoyable to me. The Women's Ministry at my church enables me to grow in the grace and truth to become a better woman.

I have seen hope and joy in myself that can only come from God. He continues to have lots of work within me through the Spirit to overcome anger, fear, shame, and doubt when they arise.

As a recent Christian, I desire to share my story of coming to faith with other disabled people, telling them about God's love, and helping them fly with their disabilities. My vision is to make the church more inclusive to those with disabilities. My goal is to educate others on how to welcome them and make church a more enjoyable experience rather than making them feel judged or labeled. After all, we're just like you — composed of body, mind and spirit. A disabled body or mind doesn't mean a spiritual disability to know and serve God.

CHAPTER 2

UNIQUELY GIFTED

By: Andrew J. Jonkman

Virginia, USA

This is my story of being uniquely gifted. My challenges and overcoming them, struggles and accomplishments, and perseverance, all with the grace of God.

My name is Andrew Jacob Jonkman, and I was born on June 2nd, 1982, at Brantford General Hospital (Ontario, Canada) to Andy and Jenny Jonkman, weighing 2lbs and 2oz. I was born at twenty-seven weeks, thirteen weeks early. Shortly after I was born, I had to be transferred to the Toronto Hospital of Sick Kids. While in transport, a doctor had to hand-squeeze oxygen the entire time; to keep me alive. I supposedly could fit in the palm of my dad's hand, and his wedding ring could go all the way up my leg. Due to losing oxygen at some point during the delivery, I was born with cerebral palsy (CP) and a chronic lung condition. Because of this, I was on oxygen for nine months when I came home.

Initially, my parents were told I might be blind and never be able to walk; but thankfully, I gained my vision and could walk, although I have some trouble with walking and my balance. I stayed in Sick Kids for four and a half months and eventually was able to come home on October 15th.

Being in the hospital was tough for my parents. They made the one-hour drive every day even while my dad had just started his own construction business.

—

Both my parents are hard workers and would often push me along as I grew up. I have four younger siblings: two brothers and two sisters, but my parents tried not to treat me any differently than them. We all had chores, mainly because we lived out in the country. We were taught the Bible and brought up in a loving Christian home. My family has supported me in all my endeavors throughout my life. What's important is that in God's eyes, we are all equal, and even though sin has brought disabilities into this life, God has a plan for each of us; someday, there will be no pain or disability. This has greatly helped me as I often ask myself, "Why me?" when I see the things I can't do with my classmates or friends. But I realize God does have a special plan for me.

At first, growing up wasn't too different from kids without CP. I was the oldest in my family, and my next brother was two years younger, so I had the 'older' advantage for many years. We also had plenty of cousins to play with. As I grew older, though, things became more difficult. My hamstrings tightened up in my legs and began to hinder my walking more. Now my younger siblings and cousins could surpass me in running and sports.

In Grade four, I had surgery on my hamstrings to lengthen them and had both legs in a cast with a bar in between. My mom made pants that snapped up on the sides, and I went to school and would lie on a bed during class. The school did come hard for me, but with remedial aid in elementary and extra tutoring from my mom, I could stay with my class from K-12.

I received the Amity Goodwill Award in high school, awarded to those with disabilities who can overcome barriers. While I was still in high school, I was also diagnosed with Crohn's disease.

I found this to be a big challenge as it was a lot of trial and error as to what I could eat that wouldn't trigger a flare and also causes frequent and urgent trips to the bathroom. In 2013, I underwent a bowel resection and am still on fairly extensive medication to help combat these struggles.

I love sports! Specifically, it was often amiss that I couldn't skate or keep up with the others in hockey.

Eventually, when I was eleven, we found sledge hockey. I played organized sledge hockey for eighteen years. Sledge hockey is where you sit on a sled with skate blades on the bottom.

You have two small sticks, and on one end of the stick is a blade; on the other is a pick to help you move. Sledge hockey is a paralympic sport and allowed me to be on equal footing with others.

My dad and brother could also play, allowing us to play together. As a family, we typically didn't play many organized sports. Still, as sledge hockey allowed me to play, our family banded together and traveled all over Ontario and even as far as New York.

I am thankful for being able to experience these times, especially when you got to play tournaments and stay over with the team. I would also try to have our friends and cousins get on a sledge once a year. It felt good to do circles around them for once!

I also played Challenger baseball in the summer. I got to enjoy a trip to Cooperstown, NY, U. where the team got to be involved with the annual Hall of Fame ceremonies, including playing on the famous Doubleday Field and visiting the Hall of Fame.

It is important to not always dwell on what you can't do but enjoy the opportunities and blessings you can do.

In 2010, my brother and I attended the Paralympics in Vancouver. Our highlight was the Canada Sledge Hockey Team. At the first game we went to, we met one of the player's parents, who we played sledge hockey against in our hometown. He invited us to Team Canada's room after the games to enjoy some particular time with the team. My brother and I enjoyed the Paralympics and noticed one big difference from the regular Olympics. Every time you see someone come down the ski slope with one leg or blind with a guide, you cheer because you think everyone is fantastic, whether they are on the podium or not. When you watch the regular Olympics, you only care about the fastest ones. It brings us back to the reality that every person is special and unique.

While my feet don't move as quickly as an able-bodied person, my parents pushed me to go for my driver's license. There was concern if I would be able to react quickly enough or if I would need hand controls, but driving turned out quite well. I have had a couple of fender benders, but nothing too severe, and I have even been able to work as an Uber and Lyft driver for a while. Driving opened doors for me and helped my Mom not be a full-time taxi driver!

In 2000, I graduated from high school. I then attended Mohawk College in Hamilton, Ontario, where I earned my Associates Degree in Enterprise Business, originally thinking of getting into marketing or something similar.

Finding employment was difficult as I could only really work an office job. For someone with a physical disability, most employers didn't see that as attractive and thought I would be unable to do the job successfully.

As my family is construction-oriented, I eventually went to school for drafting; after several part-time jobs, I found full-time employment as a draftsman for an engineering firm close to my home in Brantford, Ontario. I did this for several years until I moved to Virginia, United States.

In Virginia, I also found it tough to get a job. I ended up taking a job as a life insurance salesman. I did the training and collectively spent a year without making many sales as a commission-based job. After a year, I became a Life Insurance Salesman at a call center. Now my year of cold calling, without any sales, proved quite valuable, and I soon became one of the top salesmen and had been doing this ever since. I found this quite providential that I got into life insurance in the first place, as it's very different from drafting and construction. Again, God sometimes has a way of leading us down a path we might not have picked; but He knows best.

As I grew up, I didn't date. There were a couple of girls I was interested in, but they weren't interested in me. My parents built an apartment above their garage, and I 'moved out.'

In early 2014, I met a special lady on a Christian dating website. After much phone dating and visits, we were engaged on New Year's Day, 2015, and were married a year later. As my future wife lived in Virginia and my breathing difficulties were somewhat eased by warmer weather, I decided to leave my family and my support group, move down to Virginia and start over.

While this was an extremely challenging decision, I felt that God would enable me to start over and have a wonderful woman to share my life with was a tremendous blessing. As noted above, it wasn't all easy to start.

Finding a job was challenging and a bit taxing on our marriage as I felt the responsibility of a husband to provide. The missing family was big, but we eventually found a church that we thought we could belong to, and that also became like family. We also got a lovely border terrier who helps keep me active and can be challenging to walk.

Moving to Virginia and getting married was a significant change; there is a bigger one still. The most significant change in my life came spiritually and mentally in May 2009. Until this point in my life, I had been very self-conscious about how I perceived myself and how others perceived me, and I always took the 'pity party' road. I used this thinking pattern not to apply myself to my schoolwork as I figured that because of my disability, I could get away from doing my homework, which I now very much regret. I also usually made sure to stay at the back while walking as I was very self-conscious about how I walked and usually declined invitations to play certain sports with others. Even though I grew up in a Christian home, I could never accept my disability and would always question God, asking, "Why me?"

In May 2009, a pastor, a close friend, and a spiritual mentor told me something that will always stick with me: *"Andrew, you are not disabled, but rather uniquely gifted."* My motto in life now is based on 2 Corinthians 12:9-10. *"But He [God] said to me, 'My grace is sufficient for you, for my power is made perfect in weakness. Therefore, I will boast all the more of my weaknesses so that the power of Christ may rest upon me. For the sake of Christ, then, I am content with weakness . . . For when I am weak, then am I strong."*

At this moment, I realized that although I may not be able to walk 'normally' like others or do certain things, that does not mean that I am no less of a person than anyone else.

Strangers may still look away or give me strange stares, but God has given me certain abilities that I may be able to do and others may not be able to do (e.g. playing sledge hockey). I have an extensive supportive and loving group of family and friends who treat me normally and not like I should be a social cast-off. Now I have gained greater self-confidence because I do not care what other people think of how I look or walk or whether I can do certain tasks.

Only how God views us matters, as he looks inside at the heart and not at a person's outward appearance.

To all you parents or soon-to-be-parents who are reading this and are worried about what your child is, or will be, born with a mental or physical abnormality — if you feel lost or concerned that your child will live with a stigma or will not be able to function normally — take heart, knowing that they will have unique gifts. It will feel natural to feel sad about your child's condition and the care they need, but there will be a time in your life when you see your child's unique abilities shine through, regardless of how insignificant they may seem to others. One of my greatest joys is telling others not only about what God has done for me but also how He has blessed me by giving me my cerebral palsy and being able to be a shining example of living life to its fullest to His glory.

I pray that this personal testimony may show how the riches of God and how life is only complete in knowing him, whether you have Cerebral Palsy or not.

CHAPTER 3

WATCH ME BLOOM!

By: Benjamin H. Bloom

Florida, USA

In April 1975, in Manchester, United Kingdom, I was about to meet my parents for the first time when my life transformed into a nightmare. I was born dead. There was a vast under qualification among those who delivered me. Medical mistakes contributed to my CP as I did not receive enough oxygen.

Growing up with cerebral palsy was extremely challenging. As a result of my intelligence, specialists recommended that my parents enrol me in a regular school. In my early childhood, I thrived until my CP's severity became apparent at the age of ten. It caught my attention that other kids were pointing, laughing, and staring at me. Because of these social problems, my academic progress was hampered, and I soon found myself at the bottom of my class. Despite my struggles in high school, I managed to earn a master's degree later in life. While I had a couple of friends, I was jealous of the social circle my siblings were in.

There was a lot of stress during my teenage years. I have attempted suicide a couple of times by jumping out of windows or cutting my wrists.

Even though psychiatrists and psychologists came and went, it felt as if no one understood what I was going through. There was an accusation that I was seeking attention from everyone.

The loneliness resulted from not being able to form a supportive social circle. My whole life had been spent in non-disabled societal settings, so I was resistant to socializing with other disabled kids. Now that I look back on it, I realize this was a mistake.

Despite the obstacles cerebral palsy put in my path, I lived in the UK as a child; I moved to Israel at fourteen, then attended St. John's College in Annapolis, Maryland, USA, in 1994 at the age of eighteen. I flew to America by myself and settled in quickly to college life, studying the Great Books program, reading Plato and Homer in Greek, Pascal and Descartes in French, as well as translations of the leading philosophers of the western world, such as Hobbes, Kant, Leibniz, Hegel and Freud. I thrived in an intense academic environment. My thesis dealt with the Aristotelian foundation of Euclid's definitions in his "Elements."

With a BA in philosophy and an MFA in English, I earned my degree from the University of Miami in 2004. In 2010, I published my first book, Tongue Twister, which did quite well. My book has been read in bookstores and college campuses across the country, and I hope to write another soon.

While I was a teenager, I did not have many friends or girlfriends. In my mind, doubts were sown early on regarding my chances of finding a girlfriend, let alone a wife and children.

Match and eHarmony were the two most prominent online dating sites in the mid-2000s. When I joined eHarmony, I found the most "unCP" photo I had. I wanted to look as normal as possible on my profile. I contacted my future wife and made her laugh online. I had difficulty deciding when and how to tell her about my CP. By the time I told her, it wasn't relevant since we already shared intellectual and emotional bonds.

My wife, Terry, is the glue that holds our family together. As with any couple, we have problems. Although I am less able to help out now that I am older, we are still going strong after fifteen years. My ageing makes us encounter more problems, which most often have to be solved by her. Disagreement and heartache are constant sources of conflict.

Fatherhood has been one of my greatest blessings. To the moon and back, I love my girls. It broke my heart when my girls were younger, and I was asked if I was their uncle. People were shocked when they found out that I was their father. They had no ill intent; it was just that society had made assumptions about people with cerebral palsy. Since childhood, I have always enjoyed addressing society's general misconceptions about cerebral palsy and disability.

Intramural sports like football, soccer, basketball, and croquet allowed me to compete to my full potential! During college, I also took part in table tennis tournaments. In 2001, I participated in the CP-ISRA world games in Nottingham, UK, winning the silver medal. However, the game of Scrabble has fascinated me since I was thirteen years old. In the following years, I played competitive tournaments. With thirty-two years of experience, I am the top-rated player in Connecticut.

Through Scrabble, I have had the opportunity to play in tournaments all over the country and in countries such as Israel, Turkey, Norway, and Italy. The recognition I receive at tournaments and my celebrity status within the competitive Scrabble community mean a lot to me.

Despite the cliché, I would encourage others with CP to never give up. The struggles we face are much greater than those faced by others.

There is always an advantage stacked against us. Even though depression, doubt, and anger will always be with us, we can still have a relatively normal, happy life if we have a positive long-term outlook.

CHAPTER 4

COUNTER BALANCING

By: Cassie Liviero

Ontario, Canada

A note to the reader, as I share my story, I will not be giving tips on how we can be more diversely inclusive to individuals that have physical (dis)Abilities and/or mental health concerns. I will not provide answers that require a simple box to be checked off, and I refuse to help able-bodied individuals feel comfortable or re-assured with my (dis)Ability. I want the able-bodied to feel unsettled so that they examine their values and assumptions. Unfortunately, there is no course on how to be compassionate, but many people would benefit from examining their core values and what they put out to the world.

The purpose of exploring a bit about my childhood at the beginning of my story is to show the stark contrast between emotional states and my thoughts and feelings.

My childhood feelings are still present within me today. However, they are part of a complex web of oppressive structures, varied relationships and maturity. The reader will see that I analyze my childhood experiences from an adult lens.

In the social work profession, it is easy to combine the human experience into a set of theories that seem to fit the individual into tangible boxes that can be checked off.

Writing about my childhood is challenging, as I don't remember much of it myself. It is essential to point out that (dis)Ability focuses a lot on the biomedical stance; however, when I was a child, I was like any other child my age.

Meaning that my interests were diverse. There was a lot of planning around accessibility and being mindful that I could participate meaningfully in all activities. It is not that I was shocked when I heard other (dis)Ability discourses; I just knew there were different ways of doing things.

I believe that my parents felt that it was their place to deal with all the responsibilities that came with having a (dis)Abled child and that I should be a child. I grew up with many opportunities to be "normal." I don't just mean "normal" in terms of corrective surgeries, but "normal" in the sense of living and enjoying childhood, experiencing family vacations, joining different sports and clubs and having many opportunities to spend time with friends. I did undergo corrective surgery, but (dis)Ability was not the main focus of my childhood. During my surgeries, my Dad drew a scene from Winnie the Pooh on my cast. This was a bonding experience that I will always cherish.

(Dis)Ability was not the main focus of my family, I received the resources I needed, but their concern was more on experiences and bonding. My family never took much from the system, as my parents saw me as their child and not as a financial benefit. A lot of my childhood I can recount doesn't come from actual memories but from retold stories and learnt values.

I had friends that were (dis)Abled, isolated and shunned; that was not my experience. My parents didn't talk much about my experiences as a young child in school, but they advocated for me in any challenges I faced.

My parents felt that I was their responsibility and that it was nobody else's business how we lived our life. I did have many physical therapists as well as occupational therapists whose goal was to fix me. My parents treated every opportunity as not a fixed perspective but an avenue to open up different spaces in my life that could improve the overall quality of my existence. I had access to after-school programs that would focus on physical exercise. I did therapeutic horseback riding; I participated in (dis)Abled skiing and Girl Guides, which promotes the empowerment of young girls.

Despite my family's worldview, there were always the parents that felt it necessary to infuse their opinion regarding (dis)Ability and the "burden" of taking me on family vacations. When I was young I had a documentary done on me called" Animal Magnetism." This was a documentary less about my (dis)Ability and more about the connection between my service dog Opal and me. I do not remember how or why we were contacted about doing this documentary, but it was more important to me to share my relationship with Opal. I felt that having her companionship transcended all (dis)Ability differences I was facing when you bond with an animal, the bond is unconditional.

University was a huge milestone that symbolized achievement and independence. During university, in my one position as (dis)Ability awareness coordinator, my chair broke down, and I had to use a manual chair that needed to be pushed around. I asked for help getting around and was told that this wasn't within my personal assistant job description and she wouldn't be able to help me. Even though she was there to meet and accommodate my diversity needs within the workplace. They considered my need for this support a "grey area."

Mental health professionals have told me that if I think positively, I can walk one day; others have blatantly told me I'm mislabeling my feelings and creating my state of mind. They label my feelings with low intensity, such as sad and low, versus suicidal and desperate.

There is a vast difference between grief and grievances in the (dis)Ability world. Grievances allow impatience, while grief requires patience. The counterbalancing approach fits exceptionally well with my life narratives. This method is a balance scale where the goal is to strive for an amicable solution to any situation. Counterbalancing is a perfect way to move away from black-and-white or either-or thinking regarding (dis)Ability.

When I engaged in this approach as a child, I was seen as inspirational, undefeatable and invincible. The praise I received significantly impacted my ability to please my parents and other people on my medical team. Counterbalancing has also been a considerable protection mechanism for me. As a child, I didn't feel this to be the case, as I received positive attention around physical performance. My role then was maintaining function while engaging in enjoyment with friends and family. I kept my environment varied with many things to do. However, the professional services provided to me were focused on physical rehabilitation. Therefore, anything I did socially had to be found by my family members and maintained around physical function if we wanted to keep receiving any service. This shows that function isn't all that should matter; however, at that point in time, this made me eligible for assistance, as my functional abilities were impaired.

Counterbalancing has been a way for the able-bodied population to relate to me and also a way for me to relate to them.

This maintained the illusion of reciprocity and mutual in relationships; I behaved in a way that fit the broken/fixed continuum. Therefore, able-bodied others could fulfill their role of helping me physically and cognitively transform. As I got older, I felt like I took up too much space in the world, as my life experiences and feelings were incongruent with what society considered acceptable. It is important for the reader to understand that as a child, I used counterbalancing to comply with expectations and create a person separate from my (dis)Ability. As an adult, I use it for survival and to maintain a sense of belonging. In my experience, counterbalancing has always resulted in a loss for me in some way. I often describe my experiences as an unzipping process or the act of putting on and taking off skin-coloured bodysuits, depending on the context. "The teeth of the zipper symbolize the relationships that I have to pull together to make "the zipper" function as I would like it to.

This is another reason I use counterbalancing to stop the metaphorical zipper from catching. I also use this metaphorical zipper as an invisible force of protection that keeps out negative thoughts and feelings. I use counterbalancing as a strategy to support my values. The ability I have to self-express is one counterbalancing method I use.

Expression is used to fill in the gaps where functionality doesn't serve me as it should. I struggle when individuals don't take my expression seriously because I don't have a lot of backup storage. Like iron deficiencies, your body uses iron stored in your red blood cells if you become low; this is like a rescue remedy.

My ability to express myself is also a rescue remedy that counteracts the emotional assaults of the able-bodied world.

When people do not listen to what I have to say or take me seriously, I feel like my rescue remedies are depleted.

All I have left as a protection mechanism is my body, which becomes a weakened force of reliability and depends on people's physical abilities. For example, I express myself through writing and without a scribe, I would not be able to accomplish this. I am trying to counterbalance fear and uncertainty with structure, as it gives me a sense of control over my surroundings.

There are times when counterbalancing does not work in my favour and benefits "the other." Some people use counterbalancing as a mechanism to regulate their internal emotions, so I use it to control my external environment. Counterbalancing can indeed exhaust me. However, it is also true that counterbalancing is only possible because of my strong mental capacity to express myself.

To explain further, my physical body can only give me so much, so my ability to express, navigate and negotiate situations comes from my other senses and abilities to fill in the gaps for what my body cannot do. For this reason, I am grateful for counterbalancing because I can use other strategies to replace the voids that physical (dis)Ability causes me. Sometimes, these are not received well by others, causing me more stress. However, my ability to express myself remains constant, persistent and flexible in an inflexible world.

When I had a friend pass from an opioid overdose in December 2020, we both had similar experiences of feeling rejected by the world. However, as a person with a physical (dis)Ability, my actions were calculated in such a way to keep and maintain support.

I could have easily tuned out the world and chosen to self-destruct and self-medicate. However, I would have had to rely on someone else's physical ability.

I feel it is important to note that I do have solid friendships that sustain me during the good and bad times; these individuals are passionate about (dis)Ability activism and use their lived experiences to create change as they engage in authentic conversations around re constructing their self-image while finding creative ways to move through the world as it is currently structured. In my life, I have left evidence that I can proceed with and beyond my (dis)Ability; I may have to be strategic and calculated in what I do. However, I have kept the ability and need to express central importance to my well-being. In my life, I have become able to sort through relationships that fulfill specific emotional needs. I have also understood that not everyone can fulfill your needs. There is nothing wrong with holding people accountable to a certain extent.

Just as social workers are required to perform under certain codes of ethics, we should require a moral standard from humanity that encourages compassion and respect.

Regardless of our histories, we all have choices to shape and reshape who we are and how we relate to one another and the world around us.

My experience of writing this story raised complex emotions. There is always a disjuncture between what I feel about myself, and what (dis)Ability culture says about (dis)Abled people. We are tragic, broken victims of the human race in need of charity or saving.

I enjoy the healing power of story and truth and hope we shift towards using this as a measure for change in the (dis)Ability community.

There is so much more to me than my physical impairments. Unless we start looking beyond physical impairments, we are not creating a just society for anyone with any (dis)Ability. If voices truly do matter, then all voices should count. The story is not a survival story; it is one of transformation, accountability and change.

CHAPTER 5

ALWAYS BELIEVE IN YOURSELF

By: Catrina James

Connecticut, USA

My parents thought they were having another healthy child. On March 25th, 1976, I came into the world via a traumatic delivery as a premiere. I spent three months in the NICU and then my parents could finally bring me home to meet my siblings. At nine months old, I received my diagnosis of Cerebral Palsy. Well, what do you know? My birthday is now recognized as National CP Awareness Day.

A slew of medical professionals told my parents that I would never walk or talk. Physical and occupational therapy started at six months of age followed by speech therapy around one year. Ta Da, at two and a half years of age, an interesting thing happened! I said a complete sentence instead of a word and I never stopped talking since!

I have a love hate relationship with therapy. I love it because overall, I think it's helpful but I hate it because it's so time-consuming. I am so used to it now that I go with the flow, but sometimes I don't want to go!

I started preschool when my friends did. I only needed one accommodation throughout my school career, which was after I had surgeries: assistance getting to class.

In high school, I played on the color guard team which entailed twirling flags and performing tricks with a baton. I have to admit I always had an excellent group of friends.

41

The one instance that still haunts me today is when a student would trip me in the hallway and say, "Mary had a limping lamb."

I was not ambulatory when I first started walking. I crawled faster than my siblings walked. At the age of two-years-old, I started using bilateral ankle foot orthotics, which I didn't like. They always dug into my skin, never fitted just right and finding shoes was a mission. I hated the casting for these, screaming every time they took them off. I am glad that I've outgrown that stage of my life even though I suppose they helped mold me into the person I am now.

I started receiving gait analyses, which is a cool concept. This entails a therapist attaching small reflective markers and wires to every leg muscle. It uses dynamic electromyography to quantify how I move in three-dimensional space. I walk back and forth across the lab while being videotaped from both the side and front view. A physical examination is also completed at the time. Now it is even electronic and color coded. It was determined that I would be a good candidate to have surgeries so I could walk independently.

At the age of three, I began undergoing orthopedic surgeries and therapy, I was also introduced to a walker. Even though it was a challenge to get there, it was exciting to become an independent walker at eight-years-old! At the age of ten, unlike my friends, I spent my entire summer in the hospital having another series of surgeries. The beginning of that school year, there was a huge battle with the school administration! The school was not handicap accessible only having stairs so they were refusing to let me in with a wheelchair.

My classroom was on the second floor and there was not an elevator.

All I really needed was someone to stand behind me while I held the railing and climbed up the stairs while someone carried my wheelchair for me. My mother rattled them a little bit by calling the mayor and the newspaper. Thanks to my superwoman mother, the debacle got sorted out and luckily only delayed my start of the school year by a few weeks.

To this very date, I have had twenty surgeries usually on an inpatient basis. They are followed by intense physical therapy for twelve to sixteen weeks. While these surgeries are certainly not fun, it is worth it usually. Every surgery that I have had has made me better. In fact, I am preparing for one in about a month and a half. However, listen to this… insurance companies have the right to restrict the number of visits they think is medically necessary. My insurance policy only covers 30 PT visits per calendar year but I will likely require PT three times a week after the second surgery. I need three to four months after the first one. As a result of this, I think that I'll have to push that second surgery to next year. With that being said, if they do in fact recommend a surgery, via proper testing (i.e. gait analysis, MRI), physical therapy, and doctors' clinical findings, my advice to you is you should absolutely go for it because it opens up your world to be able to do more than you could before that!

On top of being in physical therapy, I have tried prescription Advil, Botox, Cortisone, Baclofen and Phenol injections. These injections stimulated my muscles with an electric stim machine. I felt like I was hit by a truck for two weeks afterwards. I participated in aquatic therapy for several years. These were private, one-on-one swim lessons with an instructor.

Through the children's hospital, I started skiing, a therapeutic activity that is so much fun. It's an adrenaline rush! I hope to get back into it after I heal from my next two surgeries. So excited!

A doctor performs a yearly checkup to make sure that my mobility and structure/stature are in a good place. Each session, they make me stretch before I hit the slopes. Skiing helps me strengthen all my muscles. Since I was ambulatory, I had regular skis and crutch-like ski poles. The poles had little skis on the ends of them so I could use them as a break when necessary; however, I eventually graduated from them.

As a ten-year-old, I also participated in a special dance class for children with disabilities. Since everyone ranged differently, they created a routine, which was a mixture of jazz and hip hop that everyone could participate in. We even performed in recitals with a real supportive audience that made it fun and exciting for all of us.

In the job search, I have experienced discrimination. One job interview took place on the second floor and when I told them that I had CP and couldn't climb stairs, they asked if that was a liability for them. Initially I worked part-time at a clothing store. After graduation, I had another series of surgeries again so I was out of work as a nanny for a while. Since then, I have worked full-time. Even though I had a long-term job at a retail store, it didn't work out as it required too much on my feet. Lucky me, I have landed two jobs in the orthopedic field and truly have been blessed!

Once I aged out of pediatrics, I received no CP care for many years. As a result of this, I started tripping and falling a lot. This is because when you tell medical professionals that you have this lifelong diagnosis, they either don't know much about it, don't want to take the risk and shy away from treating this diagnosis.

Even the orthopedic doctors that I am employed by, won't treat me!

However, they found a CP center called Weinburg to refer me to. My first appointment was professional, lasting two hours with a doctor that I absolutely adored. He took a bunch of measurements of my body, checked all my reflexes, and did X-rays to make sure he collected the key information needed to make sure that I stay ambulatory and out of a wheelchair. He referred me to a hip specialist for surgery after Botox and a hip injection didn't work. I was devastated when two years later, he retired and moved to another country to consult. His replacement has been equally helpful using his super powers to improve me.

I have been pregnant twice. The first time was a surprise! Pregnancy was rough for me because of the extra weight. It was hard on my legs! Let's not ignore the fact that it takes people who have CP three times the amount of energy to move around. Imagine adding 50 pounds to that! However, even with all the pain and agony I went through for nine months, it was worth it! I did pretty well with having a newborn and a support system. I had help when I needed it. The hardest part was getting up in the middle of the night with my son. With my daughter for the last three months, I was on bedrest because of high blood pressure. I have two great and healthy children with a normal gait and wouldn't change it for the world!

Recently, the power of social media reunited me with an elementary school classmate, Marci Silver, now speech-language pathologist. We actually went skiing together many times! We decided to begin a candid talk show on the realities of living with CP. I am a co-host with Kayla Ireland, also an individual with CP, one of Marci's previous students and now a fellow friend of both of ours.

Kayla Ireland created the name *The Inside Scoop of Living with Cerebral Palsy*. Our primary purpose is to spread awareness by interviewing professionals involved in evaluation and treatment, and other individuals who live with CP globally of all ages. We discuss the similarities and wide range of differences we experience despite having a common diagnosis.

I received my driver's license much later in life, at forty-years-old. To make this happen, I had to be cleared via another gait analysis and a repeat reflex test. They needed to make sure that if someone pulled out in front of me, I would be able to stop in time. I was also required to take ten hours of driving with a certified driving instructor from an organization called United Cerebral Palsy to make sure that I was safe to be on the road.

My advice to all who haven't been born yet with cerebral palsy and who live with it now and parents and family members of children with a diagnosis of cerebral palsy is… don't give up and believe in yourself! People are finally focusing on our abilities and not our disabilities. But don't let people tell you that you can't do something, because chances are that you can. You just have to put your mind to it!

CHAPTER 6

LIFE'S WHAT YOU MAKE IT

By: Dan Rose

Ely, United Kingdom

Let me introduce myself; my name is Dan Rose born and brought up in Altrincham, a town outside Manchester in the UK. I have Cerebral Palsy, which in my case, affects my walking, balance and eyesight. A child is formed by their surroundings and the love and nurturing of their parents. This is the case with me. My wider family, especially my parents and three brothers (who are all able-bodied), included me in everything; I was never told that I couldn't do this or that; indeed, my family encouraged me to have a go at anything I set my mind to. My family and friends sometimes used a touch of reverse psychology to get me to do something they wanted or needed me to do; they would mischievously suggest that I might not be capable of a specific task, knowing that this would achieve the completion of it, as I would be keen to show that I'm as good as the next person.

The fact I have Cerebral palsy was never really an issue; as I rarely thought about it, especially when I was young, there were so many other things to think about, such as what games my friends and I were going to play, what's on TV or the latest goings on at Manchester United.

After all, I walk with a limp, have problems with balance and have worn glasses ever since I could remember. The fact that my brothers and I sometimes approached things differently was normal to me. What was important was that it got done.

In the early 1980s, at the start of my school life, I went to a special school, and my twin brother went to the local primary school. At Pictor school (the special school), academic achievement wasn't the top priority; it was more concerned with meeting the physical and mental needs of the individual pupil. In my case, this meant physio (physical) and hydrotherapy for my legs.

Meanwhile, my twin brother, Duncan, was bringing home spelling and times tables as part of his homework. So, sitting at the table after our evening meal, we used to do them every night. At seven or eight, my mum and dad decided I needed to move to a mainstream primary school to catch up academically. Unfortunately, moving from a school where academic achievement was not a priority to a mainstream school where academic achievement was much more important was a bit of a culture shock; add to this that whilst some of the teachers were supportive, not all of them were. During this time, being disabled became an issue, not for me but for my peers, who I don't think had met a disabled person their age, and I'm not sure they knew how to deal with it. Honestly, my time at primary school was a lonely, unhappy time.

Things changed for the better when I moved to high school; for one thing, my brother and our friends from home were going and whilst I made my friends, just having him close by was a comfort. It also meant that we could chat about the characters and the goings at school. It was a real shared experience. The teachers were, on the whole, friendly and supportive and much like at home; I was included in all activities. Unlike my primary experience, my high school years were happy, and I looked forward to going every day, not just because I enjoyed learning but also because I enjoyed being with my friends and the cut and thrust of school life.

Many people say they have been bullied at school, especially those with disabilities; I was lucky I never experienced it.

During high school, I also had a couple of operations on my legs, which kept me away from class for an extended period. The operations were not pleasant, but they needed to be done as this meant that I could keep walking instead of using a wheelchair with all the limitations. Post-op, I did spend a year or so in a wheelchair; thankfully, my family and friends lugged me and my wheelchair all over the place, on and off trains and buses (in a time before accessible transport) to local shopping centres, cinemas and the like.

I remember on one occasion, we'd all trooped off to Manchester on the bus heading for the Arndale Shopping Centre; in my group, there was myself and six friends; the plan was for us all to jump in the lifts so that we could all stay together. Unfortunately, when we arrived at the Arndale, we found that the lifts were out of order so the upper floors should have been unreachable.

Being teenagers, my friends and I had other plans. We knew that my wheelchair would fit on the escalators, so we put it to the test using the escalators to get to the various floors, we did get asked by the centre via in-store radio to leave, so we did after pointing out to the centre management that the lack of lifts made it difficult for those with children in pushchairs, the elderly and the disabled. They said, "we'll fix the lift when it's fixed."

In 1992, I took my final school exams at the end of my high school journey. Having been entered into nine subjects, I was pleased to have passed them all. However, I was disappointed with the grades, which should have been better.

My parents and teachers told me how well I had done, especially as I'd been in and out of the hospital.

—

In my heart of hearts, though I was disappointed; if I had knuckled down and revised correctly, I could have achieved better grades. Knowing this, I would go to night school in years to come. Taking three subjects, I improved my grades in all of them.

As we all know, entering the world of work is a challenge for any school leaver, especially when most job adverts at the time asked for experience. How do you gain experience as a school leaver if all the vacancies are asking for experience? I decided I needed to get on the Youth Training Scheme, which enabled me to have a job, earn money and get qualifications in my work area.

I worked in the Sports Development Section at the local council, which I enjoyed. I had hoped to gain experience in organizing and supporting sporting events, but unfortunately, as the most junior person in the office, I ended up collecting the post and making the coffee which I generally spilled, a shame, I know. When not putting my excellent coffee-making expertise to the test, I worked almost exclusively on disability sports, which, whilst essential wasn't what I'd hoped for. After nine months, I'd had enough. I felt that I needed a change of direction, so I moved into the National Health Service in an administrative role.

Having been around Orthopaedic Surgery as a patient all my life, I am well-placed to emphasize with patients. My job was to pull and prepare case notes and x-rays by booking patients and making appointments. Unfortunately, I had not reckoned on the physical demands of the post; for example, it wasn't unusual for the clinics to have over 100 patients in a morning session.

Many of the patients, like myself, had a long association with the hospital, and as a result, they had multi-volume case notes and x-ray films, which were heavy. In reality, as it was my first post in the health service, I had completely underestimated the physical demands of the job given the time constraints involved. I believe people should be appointed because of their ability to do the job. Not because they tick a box on the equality questionnaire. In my view, it isn't beneficial to the employer or employee in the long run, as both parties can feel deflated.

This is true of my time in orthopaedics. I was supported, but at the time, I felt that more could have been done to support me. The truth is, the job just wasn't right for me. In November 1993, my temporary contract had run its course and come to an end. Whilst I was disappointed that my first experience of working within the NHS hadn't exactly turned out as I'd have hoped; nevertheless, it had been worthwhile because it did show that whilst some roles may not be suitable, there were plenty of admin roles which were.

First, of course, I needed to find a new job. I was now unemployed and not earning any money; luckily, I was still living with my parents, so there wasn't any financial pressure, but having spent six months earning a wage, it was a bit of a wrench to be without it. In the '90s, the internet was in its infancy, and local newspapers were still the best place to find the latest vacancies.

I began the mind-numbing, sole-destroying search for work. Like many who trudge the same path, I was applying for many jobs weekly, often never hearing more about them. As the weeks turned into months, the search continued.

One day, one job merged into another. In February, the Shaw Trust, a charity which supported disabled people at work, contacted me, offering a work experience placement at another local hospital, Trafford General, based within the Personnel Department. As I had nothing else on, I thought, why not? What have I got to lose? If nothing else, I will be kept busy for the next month or two, learn new skills and meet some interesting people, and perhaps it could lead to a job, or maybe it wouldn't. With that in mind, I continued my search for paid work during my placement.

In April 1994, I was invited to an interview at Withington Hospital, the job on offer was that of part-time Ward Clerk, an administrative role based in the hospital's Dialysis Unit where I was undertaking such tasks as filing patient records, ordering supplies and answering the phone. Dialysis patients usually attended three times a week; unfortunately, their condition meant lots of tests and treatments, which meant plenty of work for me. I enjoyed the work; unlike my previous experience, the staff were helpful and supportive.

After eighteen months or so, I felt an itch which needed scratching; once again, it was time to move on; as part of my Ward Clerk role, it was necessary to visit other departments to deliver messages or replace equipment. One of the departments I visited from time to time was the hospital's Switchboard which provided telecoms and paging services. I thought this work looked interesting, and I thought I would apply when I saw a vacancy advertised. I was invited for an interview; I don't remember the interview itself, but after not hearing anything after a couple of weeks, I assumed that I had been unsuccessful, but to check, I called the personnel department, who confirmed my suspicions.

However, less than an hour later I got a phone call from a member of the interview panel, who said that I wasn't successful, I said I know as I'd just spoken to Personnel. She then went on to say that I had come second; the chosen candidate had withdrawn, so the job was mine if I wanted it.

Slightly embarrassed as I had been a bit sharp in my answers, I accepted the offer, so my switchboard journey began. The role of a hospital telephonist is not as I had initially thought, just putting callers through to departments or people; it's more involved than that. One of the biggest tasks is promptly connecting callers to the departments or people they want using the various telephony and paging systems available.

The Telephonist uses many databases to find the information needed, provided the database is up-to-date and straight forward. The challenge comes when the information is unavailable, or things don't go to plan. This is where your knowledge and experience come to the fore, and for me, at least, is when the job becomes most interesting. Telephony may not be everybody's idea of a fulfilling career, but it's been the best for me. I have worked in NHS telephony since 1996, and I'm still there. I have done the same or similar roles in various large hospitals up and down the country; I've learnt a lot and met some fantastic people.

Like most teenagers, I had a wide circle of friends, all of whom were able-bodied. It wasn't that I made a conscious decision not to have disabled friends; it was purely because the people I hung around with were able-bodied. As always, I participated in all the things my friends did, whether going to clubs, pubs or gigs. As I have already said, the fact that I had Cerebral Palsy rarely entered my head, the only time I noticed it was when my twin brother, Duncan and our friends began dating.

The thing was, I considered myself to be "normal", and I didn't understand why girls didn't see it the same way. They often said things like "I like you as a friend," which you don't want to hear as a teenager because it doesn't get you what you want. If I was to be honest with myself, they were only doing what I did myself. Some people you find attractive, and some you don't. Relationships came and went until one day in 2014 when I had given up searching for a partner, I was speaking to a colleague at work; I had spoken to her a couple of times; we had the same sense of humour and got on really well, so it was then we met up, had a couple of drinks, and it just progressed from there.

In time, my colleague Vikkie became my wife and best friend. We have done so much together, bought a house, travelled all over the world to some unique places, and had a lot of fun along the way.

This story is my story. Yes, I have Cerebral Palsy, but it hasn't defined me; it is a part of me, only a tiny part. This story is about a British man who grew up in the '80s and '90s and, like everyone, faced some challenges along the way.

Still, as my Mum, Dad and Brothers were always telling me when I was growing up, "you can do anything you want; you just have to want it enough"

In the end, the choices we make along the way define us, not a disability. Life is what you make it.

CHAPTER 7

AN UNUSUAL JOURNEY

By: Dominic Gomez

Ontario, Canada

I have lived all my life with Cerebral Palsy due to complications during birth. As a child, I used to play the what-if game a lot: if I did not have CP, what would my life be like? Would I have more friends? Would I do better in school? Would I be the best soccer player?

As I transitioned into adulthood, I had even more questions: Will I have a job? Will I be able to live on my own? Will I have a girlfriend? Will I be a productive member of society?

Some people say everything happens for a reason, but I don't subscribe to this view. I'm not saying that I hate my life, I have a lot to be grateful for, but I think one of the primary motivators throughout my life has been not being happy with the status quo. Despite what people think, I believe that being physically disabled does not make me special and that my accomplishments do not make me inspirational. Like most people, I have had challenges and blessings. And, like most people, I have overcome some of the challenges while others remain.

To tell you a bit about myself, my mother is Canadian, and my father is Malaysian. I was born in Kuala Lumpur, Malaysia, where at the time, most people with disabilities had little support or opportunities in education.

My parents couldn't find a school willing to integrate me into a mainstream class. I, therefore, spent most of my childhood doing physical therapy and being homeschooled by my mother.

My condition meant I could not walk, had uncontrolled hand and arm movements, and could barely speak. However, I slowly improved with therapy, and when I was about five years old, I took my first independent steps and was able to walk about a year later.

When I was seven, my family underwent a life-changing event by moving overseas. Due to my father's work, we moved from Malaysia to Jordan. I was still homeschooled and doing intensive physical therapy with my mother when the headmaster of my sister's International School in Amman found out about me and wanted me to enroll. I then started a new life; I was a schoolboy! We were there for three great years. Jordan was a wonderful place to live. We traveled around the country and even went camping in a Bedouin tent where wild camels roamed! Quite the experience.

Then, my dad's work took us to Nicosia, Cyprus. We stayed there for two years, and I attended another International School. I was lagging in most subjects (except mathematics) due to my poor reading skills and had academic support during those two years.

We then moved to Copenhagen, Denmark, where we stayed for four years. The year we arrived, none of the International Schools could take me due to lack of space (I was in year seven by then and required a full-time assistant in class to take my notes, which meant I took two spots), so I had to be homeschooled again. Homeschooling was hard because we had just arrived in a new country and didn't know anybody.

You do not meet people when you are homeschooled and live in a country where you don't speak the language. I learned how to read at grade level during that period. The one-on-one sessions were very beneficial for me, so much so that I didn't need any academic support when I eventually attended regular school the following year. Only a note taker.

One great thing about Denmark is that there are a lot of activities for people with disabilities. While we lived there, I participated in a few adapted sports I had never seen before. One was El-Hockey (which is now in Canada as Volt-Hockey). It is hockey, where you sit in a low powerchair with a hockey blade in front of it. While I was not proficient in front of goal, I was a good defender. The other unusual sport was Race Running, a 3-wheel bicycle without pedals. Instead, you lean your chest on a cushion while standing and propel yourself with your feet. These activities were great for meeting people; it was just unfortunate that I didn't speak Danish well enough to communicate with my teammates as much as I would have liked.

After Denmark, we moved to the United States. Finally, a country where I could speak the language and attend the local high school. In my case, the Sleepy Hollow High School (home of the infamous Headless Horseman), north of New York City. A local school was a new experience for me. Attending a school where there was more than one class per grade! In all the international schools I have been in, there had only been, at most, twenty-five students in my entire grade. What a change!

In addition, living in an English-speaking country, it became easier for me to participate in social activities. I joined the local CP Club Friday night outings and enjoyed socializing and talking to everybody with no language barrier.

My academic strength has always been numbers. As a child, I used to help my older sister with her arithmetic homework, to my mother's horror!! So, when it was time to find a college major, I chose Statistics. I commuted for the first two years to a local university but eventually transferred to the University of Connecticut and lived on campus. What a life-changing experience this was. It was the first time I was living away from my parents. Suddenly, I had independence I never thought was possible. And for the first time, I believed that one day, I could live on my own. Looking back, deciding to go away to college and live on campus, away from home, was probably one of the best decisions of my life.

While in University, I tried to get an internship but didn't get one. I could probably have done a few things better to increase my chances of getting one, like applying to more jobs, networking more and starting my applications earlier in the term. But it is what it is.

College students who do not get internships typically get summer jobs, which was a challenge for me. Due to my physical limitations, I couldn't get a regular summer job like others my age who work as lifeguards, at a restaurant, cutting grass or answering phones. Most of my friends worked during the summer and could build up their resumes. I had nothing. I graduated with a degree in statistics and no work experience.

Upon graduating from college, I decided to pursue a Master's in Data Science. I applied to Canadian Universities since I am a Canadian citizen, and it would be easier to look for employment if I was already in the country. I enrolled at York University in Toronto. I knew this relocation could be my final one, and I was happy about that. I'm excited about the prospect of staying in one place for an extended period.

It was always difficult for me to maintain long-term friendships; I have never stayed in the same school for more than three years. At my high school graduation, I was envious as most of my friends reflected on the past twelve years spent together.

I never completed the master's because it was too hard, so I searched for work. This proved to be complicated. In addition to my lack of work experience, my speech impediment is another of my biggest barriers to employment. Even though I studied a technical field, most jobs required strong communication skills. Communication is not my strength! This was frustrating since I decided to major in statistics because numbers were my strength. I believed that I had chosen a major that I was strong in, and academically, I was strong in it, but I had yet to realize that being able to crunch numbers wouldn't be enough. I needed to be able to multitask and work under pressure while liaising with all levels of management. It was overwhelming.

In addition, I have spasticity in my arms, so it takes me longer to do tasks, even on the computer. I was, therefore, open to working part-time. Unfortunately, there were only a few entry-level part-time opportunities in Statistics.

After over a year of looking for jobs without success, I decided to retrain myself and study Bookkeeping. When looking at Bookkeeping job postings, I found more entry-level and part-time opportunities. I completed my certificate during the pandemic, and with the help of an employment agency, I managed to have a job lined up with an accounting firm before graduation. This job is perfect for me because it's remote and part-time. I am so relieved to have this job. There was a time when I thought it would never happen. I have always wanted to be a productive member of society.

I always had to rely on other people to help me throughout my life, and I still do. The difference is that now I feel like I am contributing. It took me four years after getting my BA and a change of field, but I finally have a job!

Having this job has been life-changing for me. The previous four years had been tough, to say the least, probably the most challenging period of my life. Even though I was trying to be proactive and look for opportunities during that period, life after graduation certainly did not turn out the way I envisioned when I received my bachelor's degree in 2017. I moved to a new country (from the USA to Canada) and didn't know anybody in Toronto. It is hard to make new friends when you aren't studying or working, even harder when you have a visible disability, and, on top of it all, a pandemic hit! Having a job hasn't fixed everything, but it has helped a lot.

Some people think I was lucky to have such an exciting life, living in six different countries on three continents. It was great discovering new cultures, foods, and various natural and manmade landscapes. But the truth is, it was very challenging for me. Every time we moved, we moved to a new house, school, and environment where we didn't know anybody. It always takes me time to make friends. Then, when I became comfortable in my environment, we had to move again and start over. As a result, I have had good friends wherever we have lived, but no one I am still very close to because we have moved so much, and it has been hard to put down roots. This will change now because I plan to stay in Canada.

Like everybody, I have faced many ups and downs in my life. I had some challenges. A lot of them, I have overcome. I could have tried a little bit harder for some of them. I think my life would have been better without Cerebral Palsy.

People might think I feel sorry for myself when I say that, but I don't see it that way. The truth is I don't know how my life would have been if I did not have CP, but to improve yourself, you need to be a little unhappy with your life.

I am sure the future still has some challenges for me, but now, I have a job, and I plan to move out and live on my own in the next few months. Who knows, maybe I will meet a girl…

CHAPTER 8

STOP IN THE NAME OF C.P

By: Douglas Patrick McCallum Kelly

Georgia, USA

I was born in Dundee, Scotland, in 1989. In 1993, my family moved to Duluth, Georgia. My mom told me once that I was born blue and had to be resuscitated.

During my first doctor's appointment in the Atlanta area at four, my pediatrician suspected I had cerebral palsy because I walked on my toes. She consulted her husband, a pediatric orthopedist and decided to refer me to a neurologist. He confirmed her suspicions. This answered some of my mother's questions about physical issues and idiosyncrasies.

The doctor prescribed therapy for an entire year. I had speech, occupational and physical therapy. At therapy, I learned basic skills, such as writing my name, brushing my teeth and how to walk/ run without falling. My parents put me in soccer for one year during elementary school, but I did not enjoy the activity. This was the last time I participated in any sports for years. Growing up, I had issues with loud noises, groups, and OCD. Until my senior year of high school, I was also in special education due to processing issues in reading.

I started going to the gym before school with my dad during my sophomore year. I was tired of being unable to do push-ups, pull-ups or run. My dad was an MCJROTC Instructor, so I also took those classes. On my first PFT or physical fitness test, I scored a terrible 28 out of 300.

I kept up with the gym, and by the time I graduated from high school, I had achieved 290-295 on the PFTs. The summer between my junior and senior year, I enlisted in the United States Marine Corps (Delayed Entry Program). I had some issues during boot camp at Parris Island and was discharged early on in what I thought would be my career.

Growing up with CP, even mild CP, isn't always easy; adults and other kids don't always understand that while you may look normal, your body is not normal in its daily functions. I always felt I had issues with any fine motor skills or functions. I had to learn everything at a much slower rate. I was either in second or third grade in P.E. class, and we were writing or filling out some questions on paper using the cracked cement floor as a backing for the paper. Well, I have issues writing due to the CP but also due to the cracks. The secondary teacher came over and said that "her kindergarten son could write better" and some other not-so-nice words. Well, I went home and didn't think anything of it until my neighbors in my class told my parents. My dad flew down to the school, and I never saw that teacher again. People don't always understand a disability that isn't always visible to the naked eye.

When I returned home, I started going back to the gym and realized that I enjoyed bodybuilding and pushing my body past what some had said I couldn't do. Unwittingly I was doing compression therapy for my joints which helped me deal with the sensory integration issues, loud noises, crowds, and pressures of life. I did bodybuilding for myself and did not compete for a few years. When I was about twenty, I started serious weight training.

At that time, I was taking college classes. I wanted to help others push themselves in the gym, so I began Clean & Press, a personal training/cleaning company.

I had special needs clients on the training side and found working with them to be very rewarding. In my mid-twenties, I had some health issues and combined with running my company, I stopped bodybuilding and working out.

Since the Marine Corps did not work out, I ended up releasing that I could still serve as a cop; it just took me ten years to realize that. Hoping for a change, on May 15th, 2017, at the age of twenty-eight, I was hired to be a deputy with Forsyth County Sheriff's Office. A few months before I was hired, I started going back to the gym to be in better shape or just fit for what I was hoping would be my new career. During my final interview for the department, I remember my Sheriff asked me if I had any problem with my disability and people making fun of me and having issues with me due to the CP. I politely told my Sheriff that I had no problem dealing with what I had or dealing with people about those issues.

One time working in the jail during the night shift, I was called in to do a booking at work with a somewhat disgruntled and disabled arrestee. This man was combative and also very argumentative with the other deputies. I was called in because of my history and abilities. The man started getting rowdy with me and talking about getting his lawyer involved for disability prejudice. I introduced myself and told him I had CP and that I would be working with him. He looked at me, and I could see all the anger in his eyes disappear.

That story is still talked about in jail. Another was dealing with a rather big guy who wanted to fight. I politely told him he could fight me, but here was the thing. He would lose to a cop with CP or beat a cop with CP; it was a lose-lose situation for him either way. That story is also still a jail legend. I love being able to help people due to my past experiences.

Despite weakness on my left side, I progressed, put on a good amount of muscle pretty fast, and ended up bodybuilding again but not competing. I enjoy bodybuilding because people with CP are not supposed to be able to do what I do. In August of 2018, I asked United Cerebral Palsy of Atlanta over Facebook If they knew of any people with CP who were in Law Enforcement. I had no answer from them so started doing my research. I discovered some people in the military and law enforcement with CP, but it is rare.

I am on the SRU team for the Forsyth county jail, the special response unit. On September 27th, 2019, I went to the Police Academy and graduated, becoming a Certified Police Officer; before that, I was a Jail deputy for the County. During one of the first weeks at the Academy, I got hurt during one of the morning physical training sessions. I thought nothing of it because, with CP, you tend to get injured a lot. My fellow recruits were slightly concerned about my injury, not knowing my past. My class president and vice president told my Lieutenants that I was injured. Here's the thing: during the Academy, you can be kicked out if you get hurt, so I didn't want to bring attention to this. My Lieutenants called me into their office, and I was asked to explain what had happened. I told them I was unsure if I was injured or if my CP was acting up.

Long story short, my Lieutenants were impressed that I was doing all this with CP after they had looked it up. I have so much respect for those two Lieutenants and the Sgt that helped out with the class. I still keep in contact with one of the lieutenants and am good friends with the Sgt.

After graduating, I stayed in the jail to begin the RSAT program with my Sgt. For the county Sheriff's Office, this program helps drug offenders of various histories not go to prison and work on therapies of many different types.

—

I received an MRT certification in therapy to help this program succeed. This program is enriching; I love helping the community with the drug issue and helping people get back on their feet and enjoy life.

I met my wife through one of my employees. I also own a small cleaning company. One night we were cleaning one of my contracts, and she told me about this lady, Nomiki, whom she works with at her main job. I had previously had a nasty divorce and had just poured myself into work, so she thought it would be a good idea to tell me about her friend. She told me about her Greek friend and her three-year-old son, and I wanted to meet them as soon as possible. It was love at first sight and love at first talk too. Our first date wasn't what you would expect; Nomiki came to my jail and had lunch with me in the officer dining area. That proved to me she was an extraordinary lady.

Regarding my CP, she thought my story was interesting. After a few more dates, I met her son, who soon became my son, Gabriel. My wife has always been very supportive of what I do. She does constantly stay on top of me about my various health issues.

One thing my wife and I did not think about when we got married was the possibility of not having more kids other than my unbelievably fantastic stepson. After trying to have another child for a while, we found out that I was 100% infertile. We went to the best fertility doctor in Atlanta, and he was not surprised, considering my body produces only a small amount of testosterone; on a scale of 0-1000, I produce 32.

So my doctor put me in his new study of only eight people, and after lots of injections and a while later, we found out we were having another son, Kieran.

My doctors don't know why I don't produce testosterone or am infertile, but they think my CP has something significant to do with it.

My future goals are to stay with my Sheriff's Office. I want to work for at least a few more years with the RSAT program. I am currently thinking about the areas or sections of my department I would like to try and work in. The warrant unit and being a school resource officer are high on my list. I also would like to be a part of the community relations section.

I enjoy proving people wrong about misconceptions and what the "disabled" can do in life. Working as a COP or Deputy with Cerebral Palsy isn't always easy, but it is rewarding to use what I've gone through to help others, whether they are arrested or not.

Throughout my life, my mother, Deborah Kelly, father, Charles Kelly, sister Casey Nicholson, and my wife, Nomiki Kelly, have been very supportive.

CHAPTER 9

ACHIEVING ANYTHING

By: Eva Abley

Britain's Got Talent 2002, Top Five Finalist

London, United Kingdom

When my parents were told that their child would possibly never be able to walk or ride a bike and had a chance of needing a wheelchair to get around, they felt heartbroken and destroyed. Cerebral palsy was a term my mum and dad had never heard before. It was suggested that I wouldn't achieve milestones such as walking, talking and sitting up at the time a typical toddler would. But I did.

Attending the first school was a positive experience as the children didn't understand my differences yet, and friends often surrounded me. However, when I was old enough to attend Middle School, I was unprepared for the challenges I was about to face. It mentally drained me having to put up with my peers being so unkind and socially excluding me because of my disability — they didn't understand how this was something I couldn't control. I managed to stay at Middle School until the start of year eight; then, I chose to become home-schooled. As much as I would have loved to be joining children at school, the school system had proven to me that it's not set up for anyone different in any way.

Even with the negative experiences I battled in Middle School; I didn't let them crush my personality.

That summer, we went on a family holiday to Monkey Tree, a campsite in Cornwall, where I entered a talent competition. I didn't only enter the talent show, but I won! The prize was another camping trip, but this time for free. Imagine my family's faces when I stepped on stage because they didn't even know I'd entered. This is how I won.

"Right; first off, I would like to say that if you can't understand me, it's okay. I have a disability called cerebral palsy, but it doesn't help that I was also born and raised in the Black Country.

So, let's get on with the story, it was my birthday, and my mum and dad treated me to go and see a show at the Hippodrome in Birmingham. It was to see a magic show that I was going on and on about. We were sitting in the special disabled bay, only so my parents could get a free carer pass; I mean, how tight! Honestly, the disabled seats are always the best in the house. We sat there enjoying the show, and the magician asked who had a watch. My dad and I put our hands up, and he chose me. I was astonished that I was picked and not my dad, as my dad always gets picked on because of his big bald head that shines in the spotlight.

The magician got back on track and asked for my new Apple watch. I didn't want to give it to him, but he gave me no choice. He put it in a brown paper bag, got a hammer and smashed it into millions of pieces. The show continued, but I couldn't stop worrying about my watch. The show ended, and I still didn't have my blooming watch back. I told the lady selling ice cream at the show's introduction that I wanted my watch back, and she sent me to his dressing room backstage.

I was knocking and knocking on his door. When he finally opened the door, I explained that he hadn't returned my watch.

To my surprise, he turned around and gave me a doughnut! Irritated, I insisted that I didn't want that . . . I wanted my watch. He said take one bite. I love my food so much that I couldn't resist. I put the doughnut in my mouth.

As I took the bite, you will never guess what was in it . . . JAM!" This is my favourite script; it never gets old.

Before I discovered I could entertain a crowd with my comedy, I used to create and make tie-dye T-shirts and upload photos of them on Instagram. But instead, I started to post videos of me telling my jokes. Not only did I reach 1000 followers, but the videos gained attention from researchers working for Britain's Got Talent (BGT). They kept messaging me, asking me to audition for the show. They became a pest because, at the time, we didn't think they were who they said they were. I did some investigating online and found that the researcher was genuine.

Following many conversations on the telephone with Britain's Got Talent Team, I was asked to write a script for the show auditions. The thought of having to write a script left me feeling anxious. I thought back to when I told jokes about my disability on stage at the campsite and decided to make my script about the funny experiences of being disabled. We then all sat down as a family and were able to mind map our ideas and choose which we would put in the act. I then memorised the script; not only was I prepared to make fun of my cerebral palsy, but I was also making fun of the judges, Simon Cowell, Amanda Holden, Alicia Dixon and David Walliams. Boris Johnson didn't have it easy either.

Eventually, the big day arrived, and with a car full of my excited family, we were off to London for the audition. We were asked to meet at the London Palladium, but we spent one hour on paperwork before we were allowed in.

Watching my mum fill it all in was boring, but we were directed into the lobby area of the hotel next door. This was where all the auditionees had a filmed interview. As I looked around, I could see acrobats making a human tower. I would later discover this act was The Freaks. Finally, I went into the Palladium and to my surprise, standing there was Ant and Dec! It was strange having a normal conversation with someone you'd idolised on TV for so long. After a quick chat with them, I was introduced to the stage. The theatre was packed with people and judges. I could hear them, but they were invisible to me because of the dazzling lights. As I stood on the stage, I thought I would explain why my voice sounded strange because I have cerebral palsy but also because I'm from the Black Country. The performance went very well, which Amanda Holden confirmed when I met her backstage.

What felt like a lifetime, four weeks later, I had a phone call from BGT announcing that I had made it to the semi-final. It was back to the mind map to try and write a new script. The BGT Team wants its performers to stand out and be memorable to the audience. I was surprised with a t-shirt with a pair of lips on the front and a fancy blazer over the top to wear throughout my BGT performances. I had the opportunity to design my stage background with the creative crew. I chose inspirational quotes, photos of my dog and lots of colours.

It was then back to London for the semi-finals. Remember when I told you how upset my parents were when I was a baby? Well, now they were so delighted to watch their daughter on stage my dad was crying again. This time with pride. He cried so much that he had more airtime than I did! I was amazed to be picked from the top two to go to the final. The support I received in the semi-final was overwhelming; the whole palladium was chanting 'Eva' because they all wanted me to go to the finals.

—

My following impressively increased. I have now got over 20k on Instagram and over 70k on TikTok. Even more, excitement was heading my way when Simon Cowell came on stage to congratulate me and hug me.

Then it was time for the last step of my BGT journey . . . the FINALS!!! It was the best experience and a day I will never forget. Unknown to me, I had Covid on the day of the final, but tests were unavailable until I got home. I was worried about going on stage because I had no voice and was tired. Britain's Got Talent producers told me that I would be absolutely fine. They let me sleep on the settee backstage in the dressing room and brought me a ham sandwich and a cup of tea. They said I would get "doctor theatre" when I got on stage. Doctor theatre is when you step on stage, and the excitement takes over, making you feel 100%. They were right, as I smashed it on my performance, and I had the nation in stitches again. I'm proud to say that I came in 5th place and the top female in BGT 2022.

Not only has it left me with a promising career, but I have also had the experience and opportunities that a fifteen-year-old girl would only dream about. I met many incredible famous faces along my journey, like Holly Willoughby when I was invited to the Lorraine Kelly show. I have been on many more tv shows like Sky, FYI, and I am currently filming a documentary for CBBC. I was invited to a photo shoot in London by Barnardo's charity, where I met Lydia Bright from The Only Way Is Essex.

Most weeks, I am at different places doing gigs and keeping everyone entertained. I also visited primary schools; I made a presentation about disabilities to try and spread awareness. I aim to ensure that no one suffers as I did at school.

But it's also okay if I have bad days because I'm still battling my disability behind closed doors.

Over the years, I've found my hidden talent. It has shown me that I am worthy. If I could say anything to future cerebral palsy warriors, I would say anything is possible if you don't give up on it. If you don't fit in a room of children all playing together and you're sitting alone doing work, feeling uncomfortable, show them you are so much better than they are and that you deserve respect, even if you have a disability. I know it seems ridiculous when non-disabled people tell you that when you're older, you will fit in — trust me, I hate that too — but eventually, you will find where you belong.

CHAPTER 10

THE ROLLERCOASTER THAT IS CEREBRAL PALSY

By: Gabriela Salgado

Illinois, USA

Living with Cerebral Palsy is a day-to-day cycle of determining to what degree my body will cooperate. Will it require constant verbal reminders to stay relaxed and not allow the spasticity or tone to take hold? The rollercoaster I call life has gotten bumpier with age. Medical care and equipment have become imperative to ensure that I remain as independent as possible. Unfortunately, society has other plans.

Insurance companies and the medical community consider adults with Cerebral Palsy as having peaked. With little to no expectations of improvement to our physical condition after an individual reaches the age of eighteen. As is usually the case, I tend to go against the plan people thought I should follow. Take my social life, for instance; people would be surprised to know that I was socially awkward in high school and college. High school was challenging for me socially. I was one of the few physically disabled students in a mainstream high school.

Most of my classes were centered around the typical high school curriculum. I received one period a day of special education instruction known as "Resource" to assist with subjects I struggled with. My fellow students and teachers did not know how to treat me or interact with me.

A great example occurred the first day I entered my first class. Without introducing herself, my teacher asked, "How do I teach you?" I looked at her perplexed and said, "Just like anybody else." After that exchange, I just tried to keep my head in a book and study. I was blessed to have my older sister as my assistant throughout high school. She put her education on hold to ensure I had a familiar face to help navigate high school. Her presence, especially in the early days, was invaluable as I worked to find my place in high school. Eventually, I did find my group of friends, and before I knew it, four years had gone.

At eighteen, I walked with a walker, attending monthly physical therapy appointments and preparing to graduate high school. I was leaving the protected shell of the public school system that was legally mandated to provide services to me and entering the arena of public education where services for adults with physical disabilities were few. As a child, I was brushed aside while all questions and concerns related to my disability were directed to my mother. Suddenly, people were looking at me and only me for answers to everything. She was only asked for her input when it was time to hand over the tuition money (thanks, mom!). There wasn't much adjustment, and I had to start immediately. I started reviewing my medical records and getting accustomed to speaking with various service providers on the phone.

The transition to adulthood brought with it significant anxiety. It was a crash course in "Self Advocacy 101." I saw myself becoming mentally stronger overnight to be taken seriously in a ruthless world. Society has never been ready to accommodate individuals with disabilities. I had to make it accessible to meet my needs.

Self-advocacy was just the beginning. As it turns out, no one ever considered the scenario of a physically disabled student needing to be evacuated from a building in an emergency. Until the day it happened, I was on the third floor of the main building on campus when the fire alarm went off. I pushed to the nearest stairwell. Fellow students offered to assist me down the stairs but having never attempted going down or up stairs before, I politely declined. Other students offered to stay behind until rescue arrived. Internally, I was in a panic, but I knew that I could not risk the lives of others for my own. I sat in the stairwell and waited, only to have campus police take one look at me and walk away. I was in complete shock. The alarm went off soon after that. The event turned out to be a false alarm. I returned to class as usual.

Nevertheless, I remained shocked and shaken by what had occurred. It was then that my advocacy journey started. As well as being instrumental in the development of policy and procedure. In the days, weeks and months that followed, a series of meetings with myself, the university administration and campus police led to creation of a campus-wide evacuation plan for individuals with physical disabilities. This plan was meant to ensure that students understand when and if help will arrive.

Fast forward to 2008, I graduated Cum Laude with a Bachelor's degree in education. In 2011, I earned a Master's degree specializing in the area of School Counseling. Just as I start to get comfortable somewhere, it is time to move to bigger things.

College only partially prepares you for the real world. At least for me, I left school thinking the world was mine to conquer, but the truth be told, I was just a small different fish in a vast ocean. People fear that which they know nothing about.

Meaning that I went on more interviews than I can count. All anyone ever saw was the 200-pound hunk of metal I was sitting in. No one talks about it, but individuals with disabilities work harder than their non-disabled counterparts, as individuals with disabilities have more to prove to society and themselves. We must prove that we are qualified and capable despite the physical limitations we deal with daily.

After endless rejections for gainful employment, I stopped looking. The passage of time made it harder to stay marketable to employers looking for graduates fresh out of college. I, instead, decided to make my path. It has led me in several directions, including nonprofit, public speaking and, more recently, the chapter for this book. Ultimately, I pursue the opportunities I do because I want to leave the world better than I found it.

My nonprofit work has been incredibly rewarding. In my current role, I learned about acquiring donations and sponsorships and crafting content for release to the general public. More importantly, I realised that I am capable of accomplishing so much. There is so much I have left to learn and grow within this organization.

Thank you, George and Sheila, for believing in me and giving me a chance to prove myself. It is what I have always wanted.

To my mother, who continues to be my number-one advocate and cheerleader, thank you!!! We will continue to soldier on and search for services or other opportunities for adults with Cerebral Palsy.

Society has forgotten that children with CP mature and grow into adults with Cerebral Palsy. Once that cuteness factor wears off, where do we go? What do we do?

The doctors I have seen since childhood no longer know what to do with me medically. They still see me because there is nowhere else for me to go. Not many practising physicians are familiar with treating adults with Cerebral Palsy.

For the most part, into adulthood, the main focus is pain management and maintaining a certain level of functioning.

In closing, I am simply trying to live my best life. If the pandemic has taught me anything, life is short and fleeting. Life is a struggle, but it is a necessary one. With every obstacle, I learn more about what I am capable of. I am a woman who wants what every other woman does: to live, laugh and love.

CHAPTER 11

THE CP BEAUTY QUEEN

By: Heaven Lei Ramsey

Tennessee, USA

I am a beauty queen with cerebral palsy; I am a warrior who fights to win. At age ten, this statement began my journey to becoming an advocate for cerebral palsy. As a small child, I had never realized I was different from anyone else because I had never been treated differently than anyone else in my family. I was always aware I had CP, but my family had never made a big deal out of it, and I was never told I couldn't do anything because of my disability. Of course, kids quickly pointed out the difference once I started school and was in only mainstream classes. I wore AFO braces, and I was constantly told I had broken legs and remarks were made about how slow I walked etc. At that point, I tried to hide my CP in hopes no one would notice, and I felt so alone in my disability.

I was born two months early and lacked oxygen, and a brain bleed resulted in my cerebral palsy. A brain injury causes cerebral Palsy before or near the time of birth. One in every three hundred twenty-three births in the United States will result in CP. My CP is diagnosed as mild spastic diplegia, affecting both legs. I did not walk until around age three and was diagnosed at two. I was told at one point I'd never had the stamina to walk independently through a school day and would need a mobility device. I defied those odds, and other than AFO braces, I have never used a mobility aid.

Through my journey, doctors often don't realize what determination can bring you to do. Never think the limits they place on your life define you.

My journey began on field day in fourth grade when no one would be my partner because I was slow. I was so hurt and felt so defeated that day, but I went home and realized the problem was that kids weren't taught to understand disability… not in school and not at home, and it was up to me to change this. That decision was a crossroads in my life.

That year I began searching for others who might be slightly like myself and had, through my grandmother, found others on Facebook, which began the process that changed my life. I started my awareness page, A Stairway to the Stars Heaven's Journey, with CP, and it instantly started attracting much interest. I realized by sharing my journey, I could help others, and I found the strength to accept myself just as I was. I decided at that point also to go back to pageantry because how can I tell others to follow their dreams if I don't follow my own? It was the year I learned to turn my weakness into my strength.

As a child, a lot of my childhood was spent in various forms of therapy (P.T., O.T., aquatic and horseback therapy). I went five days a week from age two to five. I truly hated this at the time, but now I am grateful for the mobility I otherwise wouldn't have had. Anything worth having takes a lot of hard work, and that's the lesson I learned through that journey. I have tried to apply that philosophy throughout my life, and I genuinely don't think I would be who I am today without it.

At age five, I stopped doing pageants when an imperfect walk became an issue. I now regret that decision, as well as the decision to try to hide my disability as a child.

The biggest problem was that kids didn't understand, and I didn't try to explain, so I would shift the topic elsewhere if asked.

Once I started explaining my CP, what it means and how it affects me, I found that it made a huge difference. I never dreamed as a small child, I would be able to accomplish any of the things I have achieved at this point. My younger self would never have dreamed of it.

In fifth grade, I was lucky enough to get a teacher interested in learning about my disability, and she helped me begin the journey of explaining it to others. I started each school year, explaining CP, what it meant and how it affected me. I also started having opportunities to speak to kindergarten and first grade, explaining disabilities to them. Kids can be taught to understand, and this prevents a lot of the bullying I went through as a child. I hope that in the future, more will be provided through education in school to make children more aware of disability and what that means because awareness brings understanding, and understanding brings acceptance.

When I decided to try pageantry again at age ten, I honestly didn't believe it would go anywhere. The statement "I am a beauty queen with cerebral palsy" wasn't technically true when I stated it. Once I found a local pageant to enter, I was very nervous because in a pageant, your walk needs to be graceful, and it's a lot more than just a pretty face. I practiced for weeks before the pageant, and to my surprise, I won my age division.

My confidence grew as a result, and I began regularly competing, no longer trying to hide my disability but embracing it by finding ways to use my personality to distract from a walk that would never be graceful.

I decided to use my pageant platform (CP Changing Perceptions) to bring awareness to people who probably wouldn't otherwise be exposed to someone with a physical disability.

Since then, I have watched pageantry grow to include special needs divisions, which has opened up a hobby I very much love to many who previously might never have completed it. It's been a blessing!

I also have struggled throughout my life with not quite fitting in anywhere…not quite disabled enough yet not completely able-bodied. I feel this is something many of us with mild disability struggle with. The journey to acceptance that I'm never going to fit into any category as the world sees it has made me a stronger, more compassionate person. I'm always going to be me; in the end, we are all unique, and I have learned to embrace this. It has been a process to get here, but I now love myself exactly as I am, as we all should. God makes no mistakes, you are who you are for a reason, and He has a purpose for each of us. Never compare yourself to anyone . . . you are perfect as you are.

Over the past nine years, I have watched CP awareness and the community grow. About eight years ago, Richelle Heath and I decided to make awareness shirts with our brand CP Dreamteam for National and World CP days that included 250 names on the back to signify no one's ever alone in their CP journey. This decision has grown into a family of CP warriors, families and caregivers united in our passion for bringing awareness. This, to me, will forever be my greatest accomplishment. In some way, I hope I have made a change for those children coming behind me so that they may not have to deal with some of the things I did as a child. That is my goal above all else.

My journey through pageantry has been challenging. For many years I couldn't find my way to move past winning local titles to advance to the state and national level titles. Many people think it takes a pretty face to win, which is false. Your walk routine, facial expressions, wardrobe, etc., have much to do with your score. Through trial and error, I found ways to improve and now hold two state-level titles and a national title (Miss US Pageantry, Miss Volunteer State, Miss Pure Sparkle Miss Tennessee, and Miss Beautiful Sunshine Rose), and I have used these titles to help bring awareness in my community.

At points in my life, I also have struggled with mental health issues, as many people with a disability do. I have had struggles with OCD and anxiety from a very young age. Through many years of therapy and after going through exposure therapy, I have learned to control these issues somewhat. This played a significant role in my choice of a college major last year, and I am currently working on getting my master's in psychology.

Many people thought living on campus would be impossible, but I successfully stayed in the dorm my freshman year and will soon return for my sophomore year. I threw myself head first into college life because I wanted to experience life without limits. I genuinely feel that we can always find our way of doing things and should not let anything hold us back.

I have also branched off into modeling, both runway and photo. I had previously been told runway modeling would not be possible, but I believe in life; we make our possibilities. If you work hard enough, never give up, and put your faith in God, the right doors will always open for you. Find your passion, believe in yourself, and never let the stigma the world puts on your disability hold you back.

Your limits are only the limits you place on yourself.

———

Never let fear or what the world might think to keep you from following your dreams. I want to experience all that life offers and don't want to look back on my life and regret anything.

In my opinion, everything happens for a reason, and each of us has a purpose. Never be ashamed of sharing your story; it might just be the thing someone out there needs to hear to know they're not alone. Each of us is unique, each of us has worth, and each of us has something to offer this world. Whatever your passion is, go after it with all you've got and shine so bright that the world sees it. You possess all you need within yourself to make your dreams come true. Don't let fear prevent you from using it!

I have met some fantastic people online and in my community through my journey. I have seen the need for more research into treatment for adults with CP. Children grow up, and all the research is focused on children. We face many unique problems that need to be looked at more closely. I have seen things advance in the past nine years, but I need more. Cerebral Palsy needs help to be brought into the national spotlight, and I hope, in some way, I've done my part to advance this. I encourage each of you to bring awareness your way! Together we can make a change in the world.

In conclusion, my advice to kids with CP is to be who they want, don't lie within the limits the world places on them. My favorite thing to do is to prove people wrong! Go out there and do it just because the world says you can't. Never feel alone in your fight. Eighteen million people worldwide also have cerebral palsy, and no two of us are the same! Be the best version of yourself that you can be, and soar with the eagles! Stay positive, and if you believe it, you can achieve it!

Much love, Heaven Lei Ramsey

—

CHAPTER 12

DON'T TELL ME NO – MIRACLES BEYOND STRUGGLES

By: Jan A. Kuta

California, USA

My Introduction to the word "No"

I believe my story began even before conception when I deleted "No" from my vocabulary. You see, it took five years before my mom could conceive me when going through labour was against all odds, given she was thought to be too "old" to bear children at thirty-five years old.

On Friday, September 2nd, 1955, it seemed as if I was ready to enter the harsh, cold world of negativity when I suddenly turned in my mother's womb. The umbilical cord wrapped around my tiny neck, starving me of life's precious oxygen, causing my heart to stop for twenty minutes. The placenta was being presented first instead of my head, known as Placenta Previa. Maybe this was an indication of the struggles and hurdles ahead of me. Afraid? Not a chance.

I was born to fight my way through obstacles that got in my way. I fought to regain my life as the doctors worked frantically to perform a C-section on my mom, totally absent of anesthesia.

They tried to cease the increasing amount of blood she was losing due to the huge incision on the entire length of her abdomen and breathed life-giving oxygen into my 7lb, 11oz body.

This was life throwing me my first roadblock. This roadblock was called Cerebral Palsy. Some may call it "disability, or" handicapped," or back then, in the 1950s, the word was "cripple", one of the three ugliest words directed to a mentally alert and capable human being.

I call it just a slight "inconvenience" or a different manner of performing daily functions and I'd go as far to state that my "inconvenience" was a blessing in disguise, as you'll discover further in my journey. This is when I didn't accept the word "NO" at the earliest stage of my life.

My Young Years

My mother wasn't new at raising children. At nine, she had babysat eight children of various ages for her next-door neighbors and had her firstborn child ten years before my birth. She was familiar with a child's development at different stages of life; then, the hospital nurses brought me to my mom at feeding time.

The nurses told my mom that I was allergic to "Mother's milk" and that she'll have to teach me how to feed from a bottle. In essence, teach me how to eat to survive before she could take me home. As usual, there were lots of visitors and well-wishers coming to see the "new arrival." My parents were elated to have a new baby daughter to keep my older brother company. As I grew into my early developing months, my parents noticed I wasn't developing the motor skills I should at the age of eight months.

My parents took me to a highly qualified pediatrician who said, "I was just a "slow" baby and would start doing normal things a baby does at that age. The word "normal' gripes me! Who is to say what or who is "normal" and not normal? No one is perfectly "normal".

Everyone has some slight seen or unseen imperfection. As my parents left the doctor's office, one of our relatives turned to my mom teary-eyed and said, you'd be better off if you placed her away in an institution. She'll never amount to anything.

My story doesn't end here.

When I was one-year old, my parents found a doctor in Chicago who specialized in Cerebral Palsy. Dr. Perlstein was the top expert in the field and was known worldwide. Dr. Perlstein explained to my parents why I couldn't eat, sit, or support myself the way most children at this age can. Most of the doctors told my parents I would never be independent. Dr. Perlstein gave my parents hope by prescribing daily at-home physical therapy, which my mom had to learn; metal knee-high leg braces with lead weights in the heels so I wouldn't walk on my toes. He explained there are five types of Cerebral Palsy.

They have a combination of Spastic and Athetoid. With Spastic, there is a degree of stiffness, affecting mainly the right side of my body and speech. With Athetoid, there is constant motion in the body; in my case, luckily, only my right arm is affected. As I grew older, I learned that I could control my movement by relaxing my muscles so it wouldn't be noticeable to others. I was very fortunate that the brain damage did not affect me mentally or did not affect any of my vital organs, such as the heart and lungs. Doctors were amazed that I had excellent hearing and eyesight, considering I was without oxygen.

My parents weren't about to give in and lose hope. They ignored what previous doctors had told them, that I would be in a wheelchair and dependent on assistance for the rest of my life.

Every night my mom would give me physical therapy and use the "crawl method" to the rhythm of crawling, meaning moving an alternate leg with the opposite arm (as in crawling but lying down). This method would someday aid in helping me learn to walk unassisted.

April 14th, 1959, at the age of three years, my parents took me to Northwestern University in Evanston, Illinois, where they had an excellent speech clinic and specially trained therapist. My speech therapy was supervised by a kind man named Mr. Love. Up until now, my speech was only slightly recognizable and was now clear and distinct.

At the age of four, I was still unable to walk unassisted or with a helping hand and braces. I could only take a few short steps before I would tire and fall on the floor to rest. On July 26th, 1959, the big day arrived! It was a bright, sunny Sunday after church. My dad put on some "polka" records on the "Hi-Fi." Mom helped me put on my braces and went into the kitchen to prepare Sunday supper. I distinctly remember that wonderful day. It was the beginning of my independence. I was grabbing onto a gold fabric armchair, pulling myself onto my wobbly thin legs, catching my balance, letting go of the chair and taking my first step, then another and another, until I was across the living room. Once I gained complete confidence in my new accomplishment, I didn't want to sit or rest that day.

Ever since I was very young, I've always set goals for my life. Probably a little of my parent's determination rubbed off on me. When you are a small child, adults always ask you, "what do you want to be when you grow up? My answer wasn't your typical "child's answer." My thoughtful reply would always be the same.

I want to fulfil five goals in my lifetime, and they are; to purchase a car, purchase a condo / home without financial assistance from my parents, have a lifetime career to support myself comfortably when I do retire, and have a soulmate to grow old with and lastly my fifth goal, is "fun", but would be a part of my childhood memories, to have a Collie dog. Collies have a very special sentiment for me. Let me elaborate briefly. One day on my Grandpa Rose's farm, I wanted to walk down by the duck pond, which was quite a distance through knee-high grass.

Grandpa's dog, a gorgeous white and tan collie named Teddy sat beside me, I grabbed hold of his thick fur, stood up and off we threaded through the sweet-smelling grass. The fantastic thing was he waited for me at the pristine pond until I wanted to return to the house.

With determination, ambition, fortitude and tenacity, you can achieve anything. Hence, case in point of how I completed my challenging goal of having a career position to be fully financially independent.

When I was finishing up to obtain my AA degree in the medical / secretarial field, I interviewed for a part-time position as a clerical assistant at a local travel agency, where I remained for thirteen years. I was paid below minimum and offered no benefits and I knew I couldn't possibly exist on these wages. I enrolled at a Regional Occupational Center and applied for computer classes hoping to obtain a sustainable position while working part-time, while improving my computer skills.

I saw an ad for a medical secretary position at a local hospital and it seemed like a perfect fit, so I applied.

The interview was arranged and the day arrived. The most important fact here, no one had been interviewed that morning.

I was greeted by a stern-looking receptionist, asking why I was there. I replied in a business-like manner.

She looked at me and snapped back, "that position has been filled." Since she probably would recognize my voice, I asked a friend to call about the position. It wasn't filled after all. So much for discrimination . . . Oh well, better things are yet to come.

Upon near completion of the computer course, the job counselor met with me and inquired if I'd like a job interview at the Lawrence Livermore National Laboratory, which was 25 miles from where I lived. This is where I nearly didn't complete my fourth and crucial goal, having a career position.

April 18th, 1995, I was hired through the Affirmative Diversity Program (AADP) as a temporary Administrative Specialist, with the understanding I would be converted to Career Status after eleven months.

I was the last disabled employee to be hired through this program.

Eleven months came and went. I Inquired as to my job status and was told they decided to convert my probation period to a Flex Term, which is equal to a five-year term. My Flex Term was dangerously arriving at the end of my time, the end of my employment and my supervisor wasn't acting upon the situation as I have seen her do with her non-disabled employees. The latter was converted to full-time career assignments with no ending date. I decided to take matters into my own hands and arranged a meeting with the Division Leader of the department I was working in (my supervisor's boss).

I thought I would work gradually up the ladder of command. A few weeks passed, and needless to say, it turned out to be fruitless and lip service.

The end date was drawing near, and I was exhausting all my options.

There was only one last person I hadn't talked with. This person permits no one entry into his office unless you have a high-security level classification and by "appointment only." The person was the Laboratory Director. With less than two weeks to the end of my term, this was my last chance to save my opportunity for a dream career. I created a portfolio containing awards, achievements, sterling performance appraisals, recognitions, and projects I was involved in throughout my "short-term," including spearheading a project, saving the Laboratory one million dollars yearly and developing an Employee Disability Awareness Program. I also included a formal letter stating that I was requesting my Temporary status be converted to Career status, as were the fellow employees hired after me.

The day arrived to proceed with my plan to go where no employee dared to go. The "Fifth Floor with the Red Entry," with huge bold letters, Q CLASSIFIED ONLY. NO ENTRY PERMITTED." I knocked courageously and was greeted by an austere stare from a crack in the door. I could feel the perspiration on the nape of my neck as the secretary inquired about my presence.

In a confident voice, I said, "I'm here to meet with Mr Anastasio." With an authoritative tone, she replied, "I'm sorry, but he is swamped and is leaving for an out-of-town meeting and will not return for two weeks." My heart sank. In two weeks, I'll be unemployed. I can't let this opportunity slip away.

With all the tenacity I could muster up, I used my professional voice and requested that she convey to Mr Anastasio that the important contents within the envelope were "time sensitive".

She mumbled something, and the door closed. As I caught my breath, I realized I did all I could. My qualifications proved I was fully qualified, just like my non-disabled workforce.

On Monday morning, my supervisor requested my presence in a meeting. Gathered around the oak oval meeting table sat the smug-looking Division Leaders, Managers and my stone-faced supervisor. As I gazed around the room, there was an eerie silence. I thought any minute, the security guards would enter and escort me to the front gate, and that would be the end. Not quite…

My supervisor slowly rose from her chair and meekly announced that I had been converted from a "Flex-Term" employee to an "FTE" career employee, meaning there wasn't any ending date. Plus, the management elevated my security classification level, enabling me to apply for a wider range of positions throughout the Laboratory. That was the pivotal point in my work career.

Since then, I have completed twenty years of full-time employment; I receive full benefits and a retirement pension. That's twenty years of driving 50 miles daily at 4:30 am, in all sorts of weather and working eleven hours daily.

With tenacity and strong will, I have accomplished four out of five life's goals:

1. I have been driving without any adaptive equipment for forty-seven years. No accidents. Paid for all my cars without financial assistance from anyone.

2. Own a condo, purchased with my finances

3. I Have been with my soulmate for thirty-eight years. Met on the "real" Love Boat)

4. Career position at the world-known Lawrence Livermore National Lab

5. Goal #5… still in the process of getting my "Teddy" (Collie)

You can achieve your dreams if you have perseverance and an unrelenting will. My story is living proof. If you, tell me NO, I will strive even harder to turn your "No" into a "Yes."

I am grateful for my parents, who didn't give up and didn't give in to what others said or allow others to determine my destiny. As I reminisce over my childhood, I thank my parents for not treating me "special" to anyone else. That made me determined to fight for what I wanted in life.

May I add a little memory here . . .

My mom and I were shopping, and a small child turned inquisitively to his mother, pointed at me and said, "Mommy, what's wrong with her"? His mother tried to quiet the child. My mom said, "No, it's all right to ask; that's how the children understand people with disabilities." After all, we all have some sort of disability, whether hidden or visible.

CHAPTER 13

THE LEGEND

By: Kayla Ireland

Connecticut, USA

My soon-to-be parents believed that starting a family was rainbows and butterflies until the delivery room was full of medical professionals. On September 25th, 1998, with the assistance of a vacuum, I exited the womb and into the world as an unconscious, full-term baby. My pediatrician performed CPR to give me my first breath of air. And as if that was not traumatic enough for my parents, an emergency transfer was initiated to another hospital better suited for my needs. I spent twelve days there in the NICU before my parents could finally bring me home.

Before my first birthday, my diagnosis was revealed: Cerebral Palsy. It was the lack of oxygen to my brain at birth. I developed seizures, too, which resulted in my secondary diagnosis: Epilepsy. The descriptions of my seizures include anything from a staring episode to a full-on grand mal seizure. Emergency medication was administered rectally for any seizure lasting longer than three minutes. Also, I had an electroencephalogram where I was sleep-deprived with electrodes glued to my scalp. This test gave my neurologist the information needed to concoct a perfect cocktail. I was on Keppra three times daily and took Clonazepam at bedtime for years. I have remained seizure-free since 2011.

Knock on some wood, please! I even successfully weaned off Keppra.

Luckily only saw a temporary increase in my spasticity while tapering. Phew! I am less irritable now, too. Oh wait, I had an isolated grand mal seizure recently.

I started receiving physical, occupational and speech therapy at one-year-old. While the extra help was necessary and beneficial, it has become a lifelong battle fighting insurance companies. It is not like dealing with Amazon Prime! There always has to be sufficient evidence ensuring medical necessity for any piece of equipment or repairs to be a so-called "covered benefit," It is not like I do not have this lifelong diagnosis!

I was immediately labeled "non-verbal." The speech therapist introduced sign language to jump-start my expressive communication. It was determined that fingerspelling was easier physically for me and more universal to teach others. I later learned how to communicate with the world through an Augmentative and Alternative Communication device. To match me with a reliable voice, I had an AAC evaluation. This assessment helped my team determine methods, devices, techniques, symbols, and/or strategies to represent and/or augment my spoken and/or written language. Initially, I had a communication device called DynaVox. It had pre-programmed grids filled with picture vocabulary, buttons to formulate sentences, and a keyboard with word prediction. Perfect, right? No. While it taught me the value of technology, voice-activated communication, and more diversity in my vocabulary, I experienced a lot of intense feelings towards my big, bulky, and expensive DynaVox.

My biggest complaint was that it constantly kept freezing, especially when I had something important to say!

Many repairs were necessary for this dinosaur, and let's not underestimate the stress.

In high school, it was suggested that I bring in my 9.4-inch iPad and use a communication application called Proloquo2Go. I prefer not to utilize the pre-program grids that are automatically provided on Proloquo2Go. It is too limiting and reminds me of the dinosaur I had. However, I take advantage of pre-programming my thoughts for any presentations, interviews, and/or conversations I participate in. After graduation, I had another AAC evaluation where I switched to the device that I still have now, a 12.9-inch iPad Pro.

I also worked with a feeding and an oral motor therapist. The muscles we learn to eat with are the muscles we learn to speak with. I had to learn techniques to help me strengthen and shape my muscles to chew and swallow, safely preventing a dangerous choking incident! Here's another evaluation to add to my list! This time it is called a Modified Barium Swallow Study. To do the test, my food is covered with barium which is disgusting. However, it allows my lips, teeth, jaw, tongue, and esophagus to show up on the X-ray so the therapist can see how my overall swallowing mechanism functions during mealtime. My mealtimes are complicated because I am at a high risk of aspiration. I have to take small bites and sips and ensure that food is on my teeth and not stuck on the roof of my mouth. Due to all these safety precautions, it takes me one hour to eat every meal. I gulp down protein shakes and milkshakes much faster.

Ordering my first manual wheelchair was our next battle. This extensive process started with a seating and mobility assessment. It allows the wheelchair company and my therapist determine what support I need.

They measure my body, observe how I move, and how my posture handles sitting in a seated position. My first wheelchair was delivered in 2002.

We had to repeat the entire process shortly after to fit me for my first power wheelchair, which was my first sense of independence. Woohoo! I received it in 2004, often getting speeding tickets in the hallways at school.

While the power wheelchair made my life much more efficient and effective in school, there was a huge problem. I had to keep it at school because our house was not accessible. My father, a construction worker, built a 5,000-square-foot, fully wheelchair-accessible house with an open floor plan and outside land adaptability. My bedroom is connected to a roll-in shower with my 'special' bath chair. I operate a quad, golf cart and snowmobile independently. I exercise in a pool and on an adaptive tricycle. Nobody except my dad envisioned all of this. To complete the project, the process was done on nights and weekends for several years with his friends. We moved in right before Christmas of 2007, finally coming home with my power wheelchair for the first time. Thank you, Dad, for your hard work, dedication, and love!

In conjunction with traditional therapies, I started participating in alternative therapies: therapeutic riding and aquatic therapy. I began therapeutic riding at a local Professional Association of Therapeutic Horsemanship certified center. Therapeutic riding is an activity that improves physical strength, facilitates sensory integration, and promotes emotional well-being through the use of the horse's movements combined with simple exercises and games. When I started riding, I needed the help of a leader and two side walkers, one of which was an occupational therapist assisting me with my poor head/neck control and weak core strength. After thirteen years, I transitioned to the elite discipline of para-dressage. It is when the horse and rider perform a test in a 20-meter by 60-meter arena that is ridden from memory and follows a prescribed pattern of movements.

Besides giving me the therapeutic benefits of riding, this challenges me to learn dressage vocabulary, patterns, and autonomy as I control an equine on my own.

We celebrated with a horse show when this amazing program turned forty years old. It was my first opportunity to ride the para-dressage test before a judge. At that event, I was surprised by my sister's dance team. I am always on the sidelines watching them, so instead, I was the sports star of the show! A reporter interviewed us. I also received the Founder's award. Riding is still the most beneficial, rewarding and adventurous activity I participate in. Now that I am an adult, I am active on many committees for this organization, mostly related to fundraising and communication. I have helped with public relations over the internet and in person. I have spent many hours helping plan events, obtaining event sponsorships, applying for grants for the organization, and being interviewed by the media.

I also participated in another alternative therapy that fulfills my life: aquatic therapy. It is when physical and occupational therapists use water and water-induced resistance. Once I gained enough strength, I carried this activity to my family's and friends' pools with a life vest, arm floaties, and a tube. Today, I only need a pool noodle attached to my life vest.

I started preschool just like my peers. I was mainstreamed with the assistance of a paraprofessional and accommodations, including a guarded keyboard, adaptive joystick, extra time, and therapies.

I participated in a variety of activities, including drama club and track. I was a member of the assemble, backstage crew, cast, and a greeter. I went on many field trips, including to Disney for drama with my now family of five.

I ran the hundred meter in my walker. Without a dry eye in the auditorium, I physically walked across the stage with the assistance of my paraprofessional at graduation. I received many awards and recognition for student of the month, National Honors Society and the superlative, most school spirited. My picture also made the local newspaper several times.

I attended the transition program, which helped me build my resume, a routine task a neurotypical being starts to do around sixteen years old. I was an administrative assistant and elementary math fact tutor for four years. As an administrative assistant, I supported the efficient operation of various offices at my high school. This included: composing professional emails, making copies, keeping record of documentation, and creating a variety of materials for events. In collaboration with the elementary math coaches, a tutoring program evolved, helping students reach their full potential by supplementing the instruction received in class. I worked with individual students one-on-one and recorded their progress. I even had my office in the high school library, acclimating me to the real-life work world. I also was a co-presenter at my town's Board of Education meeting, bringing awareness about this fantastic program. I got a standing ovation for my contributions. The pandemic interrupted my final months in the district I loved. I was devastated that I could not have a proper farewell to everyone I worked with throughout the years, including but not limited to the nurses, therapists, paraprofessionals, my bosses and students.

The college search began earlier for me than for my neurotypical peers. It was supposed to be an exciting time like all other rites of passage, but we encountered obstacles.

My determined, persistent, warrior mother called the Disability Services of community colleges, attempting to ask questions and advocate for me. Her contacts didn't always understand our situation. One questioned my mother for calling "early" on my behalf. Another college wanted my mother to pay tuition for herself because she would be "taking up a seat" in the classroom as my personal assistant. Wait, we are saving you money!

In 2017, I found my school match and enrolled to begin my college journey. I attended one in-person course with my mother for three years. In addition to all my regular supplies, we had to pack all my "special" equipment and not underestimate the hassle of inclement weather. I have been taking a combination of asynchronous and synchronous online classes since. These options allow me to access the curriculum more conveniently, in the comfort of my home, while my mother does what she needs to, checking on me periodically. I prefer to take no more than two courses each semester. It takes me longer to write an assignment as I have to figure out what I want to say and how I want to say it. Did I forget to mention that my words per minute are laboured due to my fine motor skills? I also fatigue quickly and need breaks. I am still held to the same standards that higher education demands. Absolutely no extensions are availed!

I had to take a placement test to determine which Math and English courses best suited me. I was placed into a six-credit developmental English course. Don't you know that my relationship with language is complex?

For example, if I am hungry, I sign or verbalize "eat" instead of "I want to eat" or "I am hungry." This is because, in the "nonverbal" world, one or two words equate to a whole sentence.

I waited as long as possible to take any English courses. However, despite my initial placement, my professor astoundingly informed me that I would do fine in the three-credit version of her course. I shockingly received an A in every English course I took. One of my papers was also published in The Composition Anthology.

Recently, the power of social media reunited me with my previous speech therapist, Marci Silver. We decided to begin a candid talk show on the realities of living with CP. I am a co-host with another friend with CP, Catrina James, and I created The Inside Scoop of Living with Cerebral Palsy. Our primary purpose is to spread awareness by interviewing professionals involved in evaluation and treatment and other individuals who live with CP globally of all ages. We discuss the similarities and wide range of differences we experience despite having a common diagnosis. I suggested the title because this diagnosis does not stop us from living a fun and fulfilling life!

Yes, as you have read, my hopes and dreams look vastly different from neurotypicals. A full sports, dance, and music schedule has been replaced by countless specialty physicians, weekly therapies, and various novel evaluations. Learning to drive a car became the hope of steering my wheelchair around school, the community and the home environment.

The possibility of marriage translates to the ongoing physical assistance I will always need to perform basic activities of daily living.

However, I am happy, motivated, and an active, vibrant member of society. Allow me to speak loud and proud.

I am Kayla Ireland, who loves me for me, the oldest sister, a college student, a para-equestrian, and a talk show host and while everyone thinks this is my story, this is just the framework for my own book; we have always said I need to write.

CHAPTER 14

A JOURNEY OF HATRED TO ACCEPTANCE

By: Kyle Russow

Illinois, USA

Living with Cerebral Palsy is like being on a never-ending amusement park ride. There are new twists and turns daily. I never know what the day is going to bring. Will I have enough energy, or will my legs be sore? Some days the ride is smooth; those are the days that I have to make the most of because I can do what I need to and then some. Two things for me have always been true about living with CP. The first is that it is never boring because it manifests differently daily. The second is that accepting my disability is a journey. We should start from the beginning.

I was born eight weeks early, so instead of October 4th, I arrived on August 12th, 1994. I was only 4 pounds and needed to spend six weeks in the NICU. Once I was released to go home, I was connected to some alarms to alert my parents if I stopped breathing. It's good that they had the alarm because it went off a few times until I grew stronger. It wasn't until I was nine months old that I was diagnosed with Cerebral Palsy. Before this, my mom noticed I wasn't hitting the typical milestones at a typical rate. Doctors initially waved her off and would say it would happen and to wait.

Once I was diagnosed, my parents hit the ground running to learn everything they could about CP. I had the trifecta of therapy. I was placed in speech, occupational, and physical therapy.

I was put into physical therapy at nine months and would stay there until I was seventeen.

I don't have many memories of speech therapy. I remember distinctly learning how to tie my shoes in occupational therapy. I remember enjoying O.T., a lot because it seemed more like fun than work. I didn't have the greatest relationship with physical therapy. Looking back at this period, I'm grateful for all the progress. If it wasn't for being pushed by my physical therapist, I would not have been able to transition from a wheelchair to a walker to arm crutches. I didn't understand at the time how important all of the work was and still is essential for my mobility. It just felt like work I didn't want to do. I remember crying about having to do superman. It's exactly what it sounds like. I would lay on my stomach and lift my arms and legs in the air as if I was flying. I would have to hold that position for ten seconds. At one point, the plan had me completing 100 of them. It is, to this day, my least favorite exercise. After I was released from physical therapy after high school, I didn't keep up with my exercise routine or stretching.

This came back to bite me when my left knee hurt so badly I could hardly walk. I tried to ignore the pain and pretend I was fine, but it came to a point where the problem could no longer be ignored. I finally had to call my doctor, who I hadn't seen in twelve years. I don't know if that's out of stubbornness or good luck. I was terrified I was going to need surgery. In the past, I needed surgery on my hamstrings and left ankle, so I was preparing myself for a long recovery. The decision was made to explore physical therapy again before taking drastic measures. In my head, I was expecting a journey in P.T. that could last for years, but to my humble surprise, it lasted four months.

Granted, I threw myself into P.T. head first and gave it 100 percent for the first time. Age does make a difference in seeing the big picture.

There are no shortcuts in living with CP, and there is no quick fix.

Speaking of quick fixes: Surgery is not one. As a young kid, when I was first introduced to the idea of surgery (after botox stopped working), I thought it would "fix" me because, as a kid, I didn't understand the limits of what surgery could do. Yes, it can solve an issue, but I didn't care as much as I should have to put in the effort to sustain the progress. Even while in physical therapy all those years growing up, I didn't give everything I could have.

A big part of not giving it my all was that I didn't like myself as someone with a disability. As a young child, I enjoyed having people push me around in my wheelchair, but by the time I was using arm crutches, I hated the extra attention. Maybe some of it was imagined, but it always felt as if everyone was staring at me. I felt judged and thought people were only my friends because they felt sorry for me. I can now definitely say that wasn't true because I was the best man at my best friend's wedding. We've known each other since pre-school. I wasn't an easy friend because I was so insecure that we'd stop being friends eventually. Thank you to my friends who stayed with me as I accepted my disability. I had a major breakthrough when I was finally tired of being angry. I was finally tired of keeping my guard up all of the time.

It wasn't until my sophomore year of high school, when my group of friends expanded to include multiple people with cerebral palsy, that I finally started opening up.

Finding people who are experiencing something similar to you is life-changing when up until this point, I never felt understood. My parents and brother tried to help and support me, but I was missing something.

I miss having people to whom I didn't have to explain myself all the time because they shared an understanding of falling out of nowhere and the weather affecting how well we were moving that day. These are just a couple of examples of finding people who got me and feeling free from the sadness and anger I carried with me. They were the start of letting it go.

Letting go of all the sadness and anger was like being an onion. I had to peel back the layers and bust down the walls I had built around me. To do that, I had to start being honest with how I felt. I was incredibly terrified of causing problems because I figured this would give them a reason to walk away from me if having CP wasn't a big enough reason. Besides my friend Thomas who I met in pre-school, and Janie in fourth grade, I had drifted away from a few friends. My insecurities were some of the cause because I was so insecure about building friendships I would push people away. Thankfully those who were meant to stay with me did.

I'm so grateful for developing a group of dedicated people in high school because it helped me continue to grow to turn my group of friends into an extended family. My family watched me discover who Kyle is when I began to see cerebral palsy as one of many parts of who I am. When I looked at myself in the mirror, I could see my CP. I'd see my skinny legs with my braces and arm crutches and how I walked. This was because my identity felt tied to my disability. As I made friends and became more vulnerable to those around me, I became comfortable with my CP and carved out my identity away from disability.

Once this happened, I did a complete 180. I became more outgoing, and I became an extremely positive person. Breaking through the cage I was in allowed me to have hope.

Holding onto hope can do wonders in staying positive even when it gets difficult. I want more people to discover that we are more than the struggles or difficulties we have.

This mission has led me to become a disability advocate. I make YouTube videos documenting my experiences with CP. I co-founded a student organization while getting my bachelor's degree to unite people by breaking down stereotypes around disability. I've given several talks and hosted a radio show, The CP Chronicles, with Kyle and Kristina. I want people to recognize, as I did, people who thrive with disability are people first who have so much to bring to the table. We need a seat.

My advocacy has even transferred me to a full-time job. I work with individuals with physical and developmental disabilities as a direct support professional. My job is to support them in working towards any goals they have but also help keep them living their best lives. We have a lot of fun along the way. I've been working there for over a year and working full-time for almost three months. I think having my disability has helped me immensely. I believe a bond is shared because I have a deeper understanding of certain aspects than my coworkers. I used to see my CP as a weakness, but it has become one of my greatest tools at my job. I hope every day I can show those I work with that just because you live with a disability, it doesn't mean you can't live a full life.

Living with cerebral palsy can be a struggle sometimes, and sometimes things won't work out how you want them to, but it has been a surprising journey.

At sixteen, I didn't think I would find a job that would accommodate my needs, but eleven years later, I found my place. At sixteen, I didn't think I would ever drive a car, but I passed my driver's test eleven years later. You better believe I cried when that happened.

If you're wondering, I received my license and a job offer within a month of each other. At sixteen, I didn't know if it would be possible to move out. At twenty-five, I was able to do it. I still receive a lot of help daily from my parents, but every day is a learning experience.

One aspect of my journey with CP is that sometimes it feels like I'm not progressing at all, and then there are moments of so much happening all at once. Cerebral Palsy is a rollercoaster at times, but I've gotten better at learning to enjoy the ride. That does include the bumps. I also want to use my story to show that just because something doesn't work out initially doesn't mean it is a lost cause. I have learned from my experience that with continued effort, the proper support in place, and believing in myself, I have been able to smash through my expectations for myself. I will encourage anyone reading this to set their goals and continue to aim higher.

One final note on my journey with living with and accepting my cerebral palsy that may be one of the most important. Just because I have accepted my disability, it does not mean I have it all figured out. There are days when I feel like I have no idea what I'm doing personally and professionally. There are days I'm insecure about my ability and what I can accomplish. Will people see me as more than a disabled person? Doubt is always there to show itself. When that happens, I try to remind myself that I have met great people, have a support system, have overcome more than I thought I could and that the future is mine to create. All I can ask for from myself is to give my best.

CHAPTER 15

ANOTHER DAY, ANOTHER CHALLENGE

By: Kyle N. Scott

Ontario, Canada

www.kylenscott.ca

They say the world is in your hands, but when you're living with cerebral palsy (CP), the world is as hard to hold as a basketball.

An hour before my birth in 1989, my life was in jeopardy. With my heart thumping at a critically low 33 BPM, my mother was rushed into an emergency C-section. There it was discovered that I was asphyxiating on meconium, a condition often fatal in the delivery room. Even though they managed to get me out in time, the damage had already been done.

My father, extremely concerned six days after I was released, asked a nurse what my future held. The nurse said I would never be a straight-A student and expect a C average at best. Offended, my father disregarded the insensitive remark and vowed to do everything in his power to give me every bit of love and support he could.

Quarterly checkups revealed nothing significant; the examining physicians said I was okay.

A college student studying physiotherapy and renting a room in my parents' house noticed my delayed motor skills one day and asked if he could examine me.

He concluded that I might have cerebral palsy, a term that had yet to be used to describe my situation.

By then, we had visited several specialists and doctors, and this prospect shocked my parents. Soon after, my parents took me to the Children's Developmental Rehabilitation Program (CDRP) in Hamilton, ON, where doctors ran a spasticity clinic, officially confirming at sixteen months old that I did have cerebral palsy.

From that day forward, I had to begin a journey of seeing many doctors and therapists who told my parents that I might never walk or speak normally and would have significant coordination issues. I could do nearly everything and beyond with hard work and practice. Despite having articulation issues, I began to speak when most infants do. Considering I had difficulty with pronunciation, I was determined to be understood. Balance was a major issue, so learning how to walk was an ongoing task.

At age two, I attended a special program offered by CDRP for kids with disabilities. This program was highly successful in building our self-confidence and also helping us form the best physical well-being we could achieve. We were given the tools to develop our cognitive skills and create a structure to embrace our literacy abilities. Around the age of five, I participated for three weeks in the Moira Institute Program in Oakville, ON, which enabled me to strategize a pattern to reach a pace and a centre of balance. The program was delivered by therapists who were originally from Hungary.

According to this theory, repetitive motions and movements will allow the brain to find ways to overcome limitations caused by disabilities. Eventually, I started school and began learning just like everyone else.

I participated in sports activities with my friends and joined a sports team for the disabled. I was beginning to live the life God gave me with the love and support of those around me.

I and everyone else have learned that what is normal to me may not always be normal to you.

Since kindergarten through my post-secondary education, I have been supported by educational assistants who helped me succeed and make the honour roll for four years while in high school. In college, I made it onto the Dean's Honours List and graduated as an architectural technician with the help of technology. You might be questioning my career choice, but computers have opened doors for people like me, allowing technology to become natural extensions of our bodies. I chose this career path because of my love of architectural design and my desire to build the future. The biggest challenge I face today isn't the ability to practice my trade; it's landing gainful employment.

Graduates often spread their wings and fly into their first job. Not me. Though I have a highly impressive resume highlighting my expertise, I have been turned down for thousands of positions for which I was qualified. Getting interviews hasn't been the issue. Where it goes downhill is when they find out I have cerebral palsy. I know, I don't want to be that guy that blames their disability, but time after time, every opportunity ends the same way. At first, I was open about my disability on my resume and would often take interviews with my parents present. This way, they could help translate what I was trying to say. A career counsellor eventually suggested removing information about my disability to get more bites. It didn't matter; once they heard I was wheelchair-bound and had speech articulation issues, it was game over.

Interview after interview, it became clear that workplaces weren't accessible to the disabled. I can do all these things mentally but not physically by multitasking, answering phone calls, meeting with clients, and visiting job sites.

This is a perfect example of my experience trying to break into the workplace world to gain some knowledge and skill sets to grow, and this is only a volunteer opportunity to get my foot in the door.

A year after graduating from Mohawk College, I had not found a job and became increasingly frustrated. Hence, I wanted to contact Habitat for Humanity to see what design work I could do as a volunteer. I met with the CEO and the Construction Manager. As a result of my portfolio, they were impressed and confident that I could give them some value in a real-life setting. The assignment was to design a 22' by 30' house without a garage for an expanding family with four decent-sized bedrooms (three on the second floor and one in the basement) and a dining room that could easily be converted into an additional bedroom). Several days later, the CEO emailed me, "Great job, Kyle! We are tied up with a concert tonight and a home dedication tomorrow. On Monday, we will provide you with specific feedback. For now, I wanted to let you know we were impressed!" I was thrilled with the feedback that made me feel I contributed something good to my community.

Monday had come and gone — nothing; the following week had come and gone — nothing and a month had passed — still nothing. I followed up with an email to follow up just in case (which happens often). Don't patronize me by trying to please me; be upfront, and hopefully, I can learn and prove myself. I have often wondered what they have done with it and if the drawings I provided have been implemented.

Although it might seem like I am negative or hard on myself, that is not the case. It's a road I've travelled many times before. My inner self knew how the interview would turn out. Usually, I get a generic phrase that avoids any mention of my disabilities but not my abilities.

After graduating in 2011 with no work experience, why would they hire me compared to someone fresh out of the program or with extensive experience? All I've ever needed is someone to give me a fair chance. Just one. In truth, I find it both humbling and humiliating to find myself still searching for my first real job.

We all think about the what-ifs in life, it's hard not to, but I find it difficult not to fantasize about receiving the same opportunities able-bodied individuals are given. I don't want to be bitter; I don't, but struggling with self-worth and frustration in a world not built for someone like me takes my mind to dark places.

As I transitioned into adulthood, my frustrations occasionally became complete meltdowns, leaving me emotionally exhausted. I passively watched as friends and family went from being successful in their careers to dating someone and starting their own families. These were all things I wanted to do in my life too, but I just couldn't.

I've faced many rejections, and dating has been no different. I've asked countless women for dates over the years with no luck. Online dating has been great in terms of communication and widening my social circle, but the same root problems persist. I've tried to be open and honest about my disability, even though it's a turnoff for most. I've flipped back and forth between revealing my physical disability in my profile and keeping it hidden so someone could at least get to know me before passing judgement.

However, both situations lead down the same path eventually. I can't stomach the fact that I'm viewed as a disabled man rather than a human being.

It's evident when you're told, "You're what a man should be," or "You're the most genuine guy I know." If I weren't disabled, I'd have been in a relationship because it's not my personality but my body that holds me back.

Love, intimacy, and family are all desires we have in common. Intimacy torments me, and I feel like a disadvantaged man. Many women assume I cannot perform as an able-bodied man would, and it's extremely devastating to be written off so easily. It's frustrating that someone with a disability is typically viewed as undesirable sexually. You can imagine what my mental health looks like. Now in my thirties, I hate sleeping and waking up alone. This kind of thing drives me insane. Accepting that others can enjoy each other's company without restriction is difficult.

Despite the experience of scouting thousands of women for ten years in the online dating world, it has been an ongoing exhaustion.

In the Fall of 2022, my life changed in a split second when I met Katharine, the woman of my dreams. We met through eHarmony and chatted for three weeks before our first date. A smile sent to me by Katharine led to her making the first move on me via eHarmony. In the past, women have turned me away after discovering that I have cerebral palsy, and there was no doubt I thought this was going to be another woman passing through, sadly. In the last decade, I have been on numerous dates. While there were some good ones and some bad ones, ultimately, they all were concerned about how my physical disability may affect "our" future.

Out of all the women I spoke to, one thing about Katharine caught my attention; "If it were the other way around, I would want to be treated equally as everyone else."

From that moment, I felt something special about her and was eager to meet her.

Our first date was at the world's famous coffee shop, Starbucks, on a beautiful sunny afternoon, warm enough for us to grab a table outside. Well, not knowing that this date would change my life forever. It was the best and longest date I've been on . . . FIVE DELIGHTED HOURS!!! I am happy to say that since our first date, our relationship has blossomed into something spectacular.

There is no denying that God unexpectedly blessed me with the most exceptional, sweet, and witty young woman I have ever met, who loves me for who I am. I am truly blessed to be welcomed by Katharine's family and friends with open arms, love, and laughter. I'm looking forward to creating many more memories in the years to come!

While those years searching for real love have left me with scars of rejection day after day, it didn't mean I should give up because I have a "disability." Whether you are disabled or not, we all deserve to be LOVED. My advice for everyone looking for real love is never to stop looking or give up on finding someone special — she or he is out there!

In 2011, a movie called The Change-Up was released. It was about two men at different stages in their lives swapping bodies for a time, and it got me thinking about what it would be like to trade with a non-disabled person. Do you think I would have the same opportunity if I were able-bodied? Most of you will agree that we should have access to the same opportunities as a "normal" person, but society isn't entirely built to support us.

In reality, our society places a lot of emphasis on appearance, which in my opinion, makes us neglect what's important — the inner self.

I ask everyone reading to take a moment to reflect on their current lives but imagine yourself with a disability. What sort of things do you currently take for granted? What aspects of your life would become more difficult?

This piece is not meant to paint a pitiful picture of myself or the disabled. As a result, I feel obligated to make people aware of our struggles and let them know we also desire love, intimacy, and family, just like everyone else. Despite our differences in ability, we deserve equal opportunities. I can use that pain to raise awareness of our struggles and start necessary conversations.

Reflecting on my life, I have experienced many things I could have never imagined, but I also have yet to experience many things as I wished. I can let go of some of these, and some will be engraved for life. Though this may seem selfish of me, anyone would understand and relate to this.

As history repeats itself, most of our generations start having children around the same time. Having children has always been a dream of mine. Being at that stage of my life where it's happening all around me without me being part of it causes me sadness. Despite that, it doesn't mean it won't happen! Having children of my own would be amazing, knowing it's a special gift to have one of God's blessings and carry on my family legacy, a gift I respect.

Although some of life's pleasures are not accessible to me, a part of me lives vicariously through those I love.

There is no one I'm more proud of or grateful for than my friends and cousins, especially the men who are true gentlemen, husbands and fathers, giving their families the love and respect everyone deserves. These role models have my absolute respect and support, and I admire them for it.

One of the things that has helped me over the past few years is getting involved with the children of my friends and cousins. Although I don't have children of my own yet, I can strengthen relationships with those around me. Seeing these kids grow up gives me immense joy. The fact that I am not the only one who aspires to get married or start a family does not mean that I should give up on my dream.

Living with CP is the easiest thing to accept since it's all I know physically. Despite this, it's exhausting some days, as I cannot do what I want when I want and how I want as independently as I would like, and it's difficult to accept what has been taken from me. Having said this, my village is one of my greatest saving graces; only one thing will genuinely save me: the love, support, and hope I received upon entering this world are beyond anything I could have imagined!

The one accomplishment I am incredibly proud of has been writing my memoir, In A Split Second: Living in the World with Cerebral Palsy, published articles, and served as co-author and a lead author on a collaborative book. As a member of the disabled community, I set out to demonstrate to the world that we have emotions and feelings like everyone else. There are dreams and goals that we hope to achieve no matter what our bodies look like, and I hope my memoir opens the hearts and minds of readers the world over. Truthfully, I thought I was just a disabled person working in my chosen field, not realizing that God had a different plan for me.

Authorship has exceeded my expectations in so many ways! As a result, I have made it my mission to create connections to the disabled community to inspire the generations to come to believe in themselves and not allow anyone to tell them they can't do something because they have "CP" and to offer answers and advice to parents caring for disabled children.

Has this been my calling all along? I know that God has chosen me to be an inspiration to the world, and he knows that I am willing to overcome any obstacle standing in my way and will not give up until I reach my goals.

You may not be where you thought you were going, but you will always be where you were meant to be!

CHAPTER 16

CEREBRAL PALSY AND THE POWER OF CHOICE

By: Lance Cryderman, PLY

Ontario, Canada

"I think my water just broke," Nathalie said in the clearest, unimpeded speech I had ever heard out of her mouth. So clear was her words that my eyes shot open, and I went from deep sleep to high alert within a split second. This is not supposed to be happening. We had a scheduled C-section in less than a week. I looked over and saw the fear on Nathalie's face. Tears were starting to well up in her eyes, and I knew then that I had to remain calm and strong for her.

Internally I was battling a multitude of emotions and questions. My internal dialogue was more like, "oh shit! What the fuck are we supposed to do? We are so not ready for this! What the hell were we thinking? How are we going to do this? Maybe they were all right, we're not meant to be parents; we both have cerebral palsy, for God's sake!" The fear and doubt shot down to my heart with a blunt force I had never experienced before.

Fast-forward about twenty-five minutes, I find myself at the hospital. The fear is mixed with tension and anticipation. As they were prepping Nathalie for a C-section, hospital staff started to question whether I should be able to be in the room to be at my wife's side for the birth of our child because my wheelchair had not been sterilized.

Finally, after much debate, the hospital staff relented and handed my PSW a set of scrubs, a mask, and an OR cap.

As I was wheeled into the operating room, I realized that my mother-in-law was already there and had already taken the position right next to Nathalie. She said she had to stay there to ensure that Nat didn't fall. At that moment, sitting off to the side and watching the skilled medical professionals perform the C-section systematically and methodically, time once again slowed for me. I could no longer hear anyone in the room. My entire focus shifted to my internal dialogue: "You're about to be a father! Time to get your shit together! Everything is about to change!" As I was thinking, I started to feel beads of sweat forming on my forehead and trickling down my face. Aside from that, I notice my heart beating faster than ever.

"What the hell is happening? Why is this taking so long?" I took a deep breath in, filled my lungs, and exhaled slowly and deliberately. I must've repeated that process two or three times, maybe even more. But the wait was excruciating, and I was angry and frustrated because I couldn't be there for the mother of my child as she was lying on the operating table. I was her husband, but apparently, I didn't mean much. I did everything I could to hold it together.

As I sat there trying to control my emotions, I felt utterly helpless, useless, and, truthfully, out of place. It was then that I realized this is how my father must've felt the day I was born.

There was so much uncertainty that day; all he could do was sit and wait. Now I was sitting and waiting. But, within a split second, everything changed. I heard the most beautiful sound I had ever heard in my entire life. My first-born baby girl let out her first cry as she entered the world.

At that very moment, all the fear, anger or frustration and any other emotion you can think of was replaced with an incredible unconditional love for this tiny human being that had just taken her first breath.

Tears started rolling down my cheeks, and I had to immediately stifle the typical loud cerebral palsy type of cry that probably would've scared everyone in the room. As they prepared to move Nathalie to recovery, I went into the hallway to deliver the good news to the family waiting outside. I remember taking one look at my mom, and she immediately recognized that look on my face.

Moving quickly to embrace me, she said in a low tone so no one else could hear, "Hold it together, hold it together, hold it together . . ." My very perceptive mother knew me better than anyone, and she recognized that a full-out CP cry was imminent, and that was the last thing anybody needed to hear as she embraced me, I managed to utter the words,

"We are going to do this."

To which she replied, I know you are. The experience of the birth of my first child allowed me to understand on a much more profound level how my parents must have felt as I entered the world.

***

As I sit here putting pen to paper for this chapter, or more realistically, my voice to text, that baby girl is now eighteen-years-old. To say that a lot has changed in those eighteen years would be a monumental understatement.

For starters, not long after our daughter's birth, my marriage to Nathalie ended. But don't worry; I'm not going to yammer on about my failed marriage because if there's one thing I've learned in my life, it is that failure is nothing more than an opportunity to learn and adjust and continue on the path towards progress.

I was born nearly two months premature. The day I arrived, my parents did not experience that incredible moment of hearing their newborn cry for the first time. When I entered, the room was silent; a swarm of doctors worked feverishly to stabilize me. My lungs were underdeveloped, and I was not breathing. At the time, no one knew what the lack of oxygen for such a prolonged period would mean for me.

But thankfully, I was my parents' third child, and my mother was quite confident in her ability to recognize certain developmental milestones. She started to notice that something was different around six months of age, but doctors were being very tight-lipped for whatever reason. My mother began researching childhood conditions on her own. She even went as far as to borrow a neighbour's encyclopedias — no Google in 1981. Eventually, she stumbled upon an entry that made her stop dead in her tracks. She read the several paragraphs describing this condition and knew she had found the answer. She began sharing that encyclopedia article with other people and gained confidence every time she shared it with someone.

Eventually, when I was about ten months of age, my parents finally had an appointment with the doctor. According to my mother, they were ushered into the doctor's office and exchanged pleasantries. The doctor quickly moved into a very complex discussion, full of medical terms and jargon that neither of my parents had ever heard of.

At one point during the doctor's spiel, my mother stopped mid-sentence and said, "My baby has cerebral palsy, doesn't he?" The doctor paused and finally relented with a nod, confirming what she had already known for months. The prognosis they gave was anything but stellar as well. According to the doctor, I wasn't supposed to be able to talk, walk, think for myself, feed myself, dress or do anything for myself. Ultimately, I would be reliant on others for the rest of my life. I believe they went as far as to recommend that my parents think about placing me in an institution. Thankfully, they did not take the advice or fully agree or believe the prognosis.

Early on in my life, my parents made a fundamental decision. That decision would shape the course of my life forever. They decided they were not going to let my cerebral palsy change the way they were going to raise me. Don't get me wrong, they are not fools, and they understood full well that the condition would likely impact how we did things, but they were not going to allow it to change their expectations. They were committed to giving me as normal a life as possible. They wanted me to have every opportunity to learn, grow and develop just as much as the other two children.

I know it wasn't easy for them. They had to listen to experts and other parents and decide what was valuable and what was not.

My mom was talking to my dad on the way home from a parent group meeting that evening, and she said to him, "I'm never going back there. I'm tired of listening to them talk about how awful their life is and how difficult life is for their disabled child." From then on, there would be no parent groups for my mom and dad. I believe it was decisions like these that laid the foundation of the person that I was to become.

As I got older, my relationship with cerebral palsy changed dramatically, but because of these fundamental decisions of my forward-thinking parents, I was more than ready.

In my early years in school, I spent a lot of time at the local Children's Treatment Centre (CTC), where I could receive intensive physio and occupational therapy while still receiving some academic instruction. In those early years in CTC, I experienced one of the first fundamental life lessons that have stayed with me.

It happened in the fall when I was about seven years old. I'd returned to CTC after the long summer break. Like many of my peers, I did not keep up with my physiotherapy over the summer break, and my muscles were extremely tight. So often, my first few sessions with the physiotherapist were less than pleasant upon our return. This was especially true on the dreaded "measurement day." On this day, the therapist performed stretches in various ways to determine how far I could bend at multiple joints. This was an unbearable experience.

"Do we have to?" I remember pleading with my therapist the previous year. "I know this is really going to hurt . . ." Most of the time, the experience of measurement day was exactly as I described — agonizing. However, at our CTC, we had one physiotherapist that was different from all the rest.

She had blonde shoulder-length hair, wore bright pink lipstick every day, and had a distinct and unforgettable laugh that would echo throughout the halls of the treatment centre. No matter where you were in the building — Sally's laughter could be heard from anywhere.

Sally's approach to measurement day was different. As soon as the session began, she would start a conversation with me about anything unrelated to the task at hand.

She had a way with young kids and, within minutes, would usually have me laughing about something so silly that my seven-year-old brain was no longer focusing on the stretches. I was focused on Sally's silly story, or the conversation she was having with my feet which she had decided were named Sandy and George.

Before I knew it, the measurement session and assessment were completed. Her magic was contagious, and all of we so loved her. Anyone who grew up in Sudbury and attended CTC knew her. Sadly, she passed away from cancer in 2014.

Here's the interesting part. I am now nearly forty-two years old, and to this day, whenever I experience extreme pain, I laugh hysterically instead of crying or screaming. I attribute that conditioned response to the magic of Sally.

Of course, my seven-year-old self didn't truly understand what Sally was doing. But as I got older, I started to understand more and more. Fundamentally, this experience taught me to shift my focus away from something uncomfortable yet inevitable due to cerebral palsy. What she was teaching me was that I had a fundamental choice. I could choose to focus on the negative aspects of the experience, or I could choose to focus on something else. By giving me another focal point, I learned that although cerebral palsy was going to lead to some very uncomfortable things, those things were only uncomfortable if I allowed them to be.

As years went by, I expanded the idea and decided to focus on what I could control rather than what I could not control. This helped me in the playground at school when my able-bodied peers would start teasing me. Eventually, I realized they would never stop teasing me unless I ignored them.

The ability to choose how I was going to behave or how I was going to react became my secret weapon. No matter the circumstances, I knew I was in control of one thing every time. I would always have a choice.

Ultimately, this philosophy has impacted every facet of my life. I have been fortunate enough to experience some wonderful triumphs, including completing an undergraduate degree in psychology, completing a master's degree in business administration, and becoming a Paralympian, husband, and father. Of course, my life journey is far from over, and it certainly has not been perfect. But no one's life is perfect.

No matter what life brings, I will embrace the challenge and accept it because I alone have the power to choose the course of my life, and so do you.

CHAPTER 17

"YOUR SON HAS CEREBRAL PALSY"

Maclain Agnew, written by: Brenda Agnew

Ontario, Canada

I looked at my perfect year-old son Maclain as we sat in the developmental pediatrician's office and thought, what does this mean? It was a diagnosis I had suspected for a while and had done some research on, but hearing those words was devastating. From that moment on, my life will forever be split in half, before CP and after CP.

Maclain's story started on August 2nd, 2007. I was expecting identical twin boys, and on that fateful day, we realized one of our sons had passed away in utero due to Twin to Twin Transfusion. The decision was made to deliver Maclain to save his life. He was born at twenty-nine weeks weighing in at 3lbs 7oz, with half his blood gone, underdeveloped lungs and in shock. He was also born a fighter, a survivor, and a warrior.

He spent three months in a local hospital's Neonatal Intensive Care Unit. He is learning to breathe, eat, regulate his temperature and take time to grow. He was doing great the first few days in the NICU, and we were all very optimistic that he had come through the worst of it and that we could start to move forward and heal.

Sadly on day three of life, Maclain got jaundiced. A common condition, especially in premature infants, is easily treatable using phototherapy. Left untreated, it can cause brain damage and hearing loss, and in extreme cases, it can be fatal.

Maclain was not treated for his jaundice for many reasons, including failure to update guidelines and provide a reasonable standard of care. His untreated jaundice caused Kernicterus, which resulted in his Cerebral Palsy and hearing loss. We would not receive two diagnoses until we were discharged from the NICU. This also brought with it a long legal battle to try and make things right and change how things are done with the hopes that no other family will have to go through that preventable heartbreak.

His early years were a blur of therapies, appointments, sadness, questions, worries, altered expectations and fear of the unknown. They were also full of smiles, inch stones, joy, unconditional love and wonderful learning.

The hard part about a Cerebral Palsy diagnosis is that it is all about the list of negative impacts. The things that will never happen or will be unlikely even to happen. It is often doom and gloom, with a worrisome outlook and automatic assumptions about function and the future.

We were told so many things starting with he would never hear; he would never speak, walk or sit on his own. He won't eat orally, will never be able to read, will need to be in a special classroom, and will struggle with learning. He will never be independent, have a job, or live independently. There was bad news, sad predictions and grim answers everywhere we turned.

But here is the thing. Cerebral Palsy isn't bad or sad. Yes, there can be extreme challenges that come with this diagnosis, and things may look different or need to be done in a way that isn't the same as others, but at the end of the day, it is just a diagnosis.

Maclain is amazing. He really, truly is. He has a smile that lights up the room, a personality that doesn't quit and a sense of humour that breaks down barriers.

He has taught our families, friends and the bigger community much about kindness, tolerance, perseverance, accessibility and never set limits. He has defied the odds, proven so many people wrong, and continues to amaze those who have the privilege of being in his presence. We have learned the tremendous value of small accomplishments and paying attention to how far he has come from those early days.

My son loves hard and laughs harder. He has developed lifelong dedicated friendships because of who he is and what he offers as a friend. He is obsessed with movies, video games, pop culture and chocolate. He can't get enough adventures, travelling, road trips and experiences. His friends love him for who he is and don't see his CP as anything more than a part of who he is. They embrace all that he has to offer and have never wavered in their commitment to that friendship. His friends celebrate all the awesome things he does and are as proud of him as he is of them. It is truly remarkable to witness.

After his diagnosis of being profoundly deaf, we worried immensely about his ability to communicate, and we advocated fiercely for cochlear implants. Finally, he was given that chance to hear, which changed his world. With hearing came speech, the speech we were told he would never have. And now he never stops talking. Maclain talks from when he wakes up until he goes to bed. Telling anyone who will listen about his favourite superhero or how unfair his mom is for saying no to something, telling an inappropriate joke, or giving instructions on playing a video game.

We worked hard to ensure that Maclain was part of the mainstream program at his local school and that he would have the support he needed to succeed. That part about never being able to read? He is an avid and effective reader who uses closed captioning to enjoy his favourite YouTube video when he wants a break from his cochlear implants. He is in high school now, in Grade ten and is the FIRST student in our school system to be a credit-earning student requiring full-time support. He was on the honor roll last year and is up for a subject award in Math. I bet that wasn't something they thought he could ever accomplish. He is on the school council as the school spirit rep; he attends school sporting events and helps organize awareness days and campaigns at school. He is a valued contributor to his school community, and his fellow students love having him around.

Maclain is a voracious eater. Love everything about food. It is one of his favourite pastimes. We were told he would never eat orally, and today his favourite food is steak.

We were informed that he would never have independent mobility and that using a powered wheelchair wouldn't be possible because of the severity of his CP. Well, we call his power chair the Green Machine, and he uses it by pushing switches with his feet.

He has made us better because of his love for life and his ability to face adversity with that winning smile. He gets down; we all do. Life is hard sometimes, and we don't pretend otherwise. But together, we always manage to figure it out. He has many questions about his future, and so do we, and we don't have all the answers. He wants to get married, and have a job, house, kids, and a sports car, just like most fifteen-year-old boys. And I want those for him.

He has taught us the importance of advocating for change in many ways, from accessibility to education to healthcare, societal attitudes, and how we view people with disabilities.

As I write this, we will be gearing up to celebrate World CP Day on October 6th. CELEBRATE! He has brought this day to his school, and the school board and many people will have the chance to learn more about what CP is and also what CP isn't. And we will all wear green and remember how grateful we are to have Maclain in our lives and to acknowledge that he wouldn't be the incredible individual he is were it not for his CP.

CHAPTER 18

LIMITS? NEVER HEARD OF THEM

By: Maddy Workman

Ontario, Canada

As we grow up, we go through experiences we love and experiences that leave us questioning why they happened. Growing up with CP has its ups and downs, as life generally does. Our mindset and how we deal with what we are given are important.

Three days before I was due, my mother went into labour at 1:00 am, which lasted six hours. I was born on June 6th, 2000. During the delivery, I lost my oxygen supply for thirty-forty minutes. As the doctors pulled me out, I got stuck, and they had to pop my left shoulder out to save my life. When I was six hours old, I was internally bleeding and seizing. I was barely alive with all the damage done to my vital organs, especially my brain. I had to be ventilated and have a machine breathe for me to keep me alive. I was given many drugs for various reasons. They told my parents for three days that I would likely die; if I lived, I would be mostly brain-dead.

My mother never believed them, so my family kept fighting and praying for my life. I chose not to give up but stay and fight. I had to have half of my stomach removed at four days old due to dead tissue. After that, I started to heal and slowly get stronger. I pulled my breathing tube out at two weeks old because I did not need it.

At a month old, my family brought me home on a kangaroo pump feeding machine they called my G tube. The doctors continued to tell my parents that I would never walk, talk, or even eat by mouth. I didn't hesitate to prove them wrong, as I started breastfeeding only three days after coming home. I nursed until I was well over a year old. From the day I was born, I have challenged the limits people have placed upon me, and I continue to do so today.

My favourite story from when I was little is when I got my first pony walker. I was about two years old when my physiotherapist (P.T.) brought a pony walker to my house for me to try. Before they put me in the walker, the PT told my mother not to expect much, but I had other ideas. I ran straight to the Tupperware cupboards and pulled everything out, which made a lot of noise. As I was doing this, everyone watching me started crying.

I did many types of physical therapy for most of my early childhood years to help me gain strength and independence. One of the significant therapies I did was Euro Peds, where they used a special therapy suit with bungee cords to correct my posture and help me balance. While wearing this suit, I could take seventeen steps independently when I was eight years old. Another major type of therapy was conductive education which is repetitive activities to train muscle memory in the brain. When I was eleven, I told my mom that I didn't want to do therapy anymore because I didn't feel like it was helping me anymore. I just wanted to live life and be a kid.

I vaguely remember the time I did my very first transfer all by myself. I had to go to the bathroom, but my mother did not want to take me immediately, so I gave up waiting and tried to get on myself.

I managed to get onto the toilet using the bar on the wall. Once I got on the toilet, I called my mom, excited that I just did my transfer.

I have always strived to be as independent as possible, and I have my mom to thank for that! My mom did not go easy on me as a baby and little girl. She put me on the floor with my toys just far enough out of my reach, so I had to figure out how to use my body if I wanted my toy. Fast forward to 2019, when I learned about the JACO robotic arm that would attach to the power wheelchair that I control with my joystick. I had gotten a demo when I learned it cost $40,000, but I didn't care because I knew it would change my life. I decided to set up a Go Fund Me page, and with the help of my community, I was able to purchase JACO a year later! Understand that when you have a disability, you really can't put a price on independence. We want the same things that people without disabilities wish, but we need extra support.

My whole life, I have faced many obstacles that have helped me grow and learn to advocate for myself. Whenever I had to change schools or go somewhere where I'd meet new people, I was always a little nervous because I had to train everyone and show them what I could do and advocate for myself. At Elora Public School, I was hanging out in the hall with my friends, and we had a treat. I could eat it on my own, but one of the teachers caught me and said, "you're not allowed to eat it unsupervised because it is a 'choking hazard.'" I did not listen to him and took a bite of what I was eating because that was ridiculous; they saw me differently than my friends simply because I have a disability.

When it was time for college, I, like most young adults, wanted to move out from my hometown. The only difference for me was the extra challenges that come with living independently with a disability. When deciding which college to attend, I knew I wanted to move out, but I still wanted to be close to home, so my family could get to me if needed. I decided to go to Mohawk College in Hamilton, which is forty-five minutes from my hometown. Honestly, my mom was more scared about me moving out than I was. I am currently twenty-two years old, living independently in a college residence studying architectural technology. My career goal is to help make the world more accessible, as I'm tired of not being able to go places simply because I use a wheelchair.

For most of my life, I had PSWs from the agency's come to help me with activities of daily living. Let's say that was my least favourite part about living with CP. In 2016, when I stayed at Holland Bloorview Kids Rehabilitation Hospital, my social worker thought I should apply for the Direct Funding program (DF), which is a program that gives you money to hire your personal care attendants. I'm not going to lie; the application process sucked and felt very discouraging and overwhelming. However, I'm glad I saw it through because I finally started the program in the summer of 2020, right after the pandemic began, and the program changed my life! My first hire was Michaela, who wasn't a stranger because our families used to go camping together when we were younger! My second hire was someone I didn't really like, but she quit after not too long!

Then came Michelle! She was awesome and made me laugh A LOT. I didn't want her to come over while my mom had a client at home because we could not stay quiet! Unfortunately, her husband got a job offer out of town, so they had to move away. Finally came Alanna, who was also awesome!

When I eventually returned to college after being home for two years during the pandemic, I had to hire all new workers in Hamilton. When I interview people, I'm looking for people I will get along with. Before getting DF, I had so many PSWs that I didn't feel comfortable with, so I have a good sense of whether someone is going to be a good fit. For me, it's essential that my workers feel more like friends rather than workers. It makes a difference because I want them to come and do stuff with me! This is what I think the care industry should be like for everyone because it makes such a difference in my quality of life and my happiness! I feel so lucky with the workers I've found.

Life surely isn't all sunshine and rainbows. As a young adult, I struggle with loneliness. Although I have made some great friends, none have stayed permanently. Do you know how in TV shows they often have characters that have great connections, whether they are friends or siblings? Well, I hate to say it, but it's not the reality for everyone . . . at least not me. It wasn't until grade seven that I first found and learned what true friends were. I had a group of friends I loved, and I felt it didn't matter that I had a disability. I remember I went to my friend's birthday in the winter with my manual wheelchair, and we decided to go to the store. Well, there was this one sidewalk that was not cleared. I don't even know why they decided to push me through the snow instead of going on the road, but that's what they did. They made me feel included despite our differences. We graduated from grade eight together, and those two years were the best social years of my life. Then high school came, and they slowly drifted away from me. Even my best friend from that group stopped reaching out to me but would answer me when I reached out to her. I didn't want that kind of friendship, so I stopped reaching out.

Relationships can't just be one way. I've made many friends and good connections, both with people my age and even with adults, that I thought would last forever — but I've been wrong many times. Too often, I felt like I was the only one holding my friendships together and eventually, I had to learn not to hold on so tightly. My best friend is Michaela, who I got because I started on DF. I asked if she was comfortable showering me and stuff when I interviewed her. I could tell it would be a good fit! The first day she came over, she felt like an old friend coming to visit. The only difference was she helped me shower. After I moved away to college, she stopped working with me, but despite the distance, she has continued to be there and support me through one of the most challenging times in my life! I look forward to finding a partner and creating a family full of love, joy and happiness! I am a CP warrior!

CHAPTER 19

SAM I AM

By: Samuel L. Faulk

Washington, USA

Meet two best friends who share a physical disability.

Sam Faulk has cerebral palsy on his left side and enjoys life as a depressing poet, avid reader of post-Twilight era YA novels, and works in a library. He is Righty. Sam Maupin has cerebral palsy on his right side, is a board operator for a radio station, a licensed drone pilot, and a decent enough martial artist to look scary. He is Lefty. Two Sams. Two perspectives. One disability.

If you like our story, please consider supporting our podcast:

https://anchor.fm/sam-i-am7/support

Introduction

Everyone has a story. Stories are what creates life. Without stories, we would know no history. Without stories, there would be a distinct lack of human experience. My story starts at my birth; believe me, it was a train wreck. You see, I was born early. I was expected to be born on April Fool's day, but *surprise!* My mom got the flu, and it made me sick as well.

On December 31, 1992, my mom was airlifted from our hometown of Blyn to the Swedish Medical Center in Seattle. That kinda ruined her New Year's Eve plans. Some hours later, I was born, and that was just the beginning.

143

The list of complications that occurred with my birth is rather long. I'll try and explain each one I can find. So, along with being born blue and not breathing, I had the following: Right Grade four intraventricular hemorrhage, and left grade two intraventricular hemorrhage. I had massive bleeding in my brain.

Hyaline membrane disease. Required extra help breathing. My lungs weren't fully developed. I had air pockets in my lungs, so the doctor had to go inside my lung and release the pressure. He missed. Hit an artery. I lost WAY too much blood. Only two weeks old, and they took me in for a blood transfusion. It worked, but not perfectly. I died twice on that operating table. My heart stopped beating. Flatlined. Dead. Those doctors didn't give up on me though, they kept working, and soon my heart was beating again. Bam. $201 bill for "newborn resuscitation." This happened three times. $201 a pop.

God didn't give up on me, and I have a cross-shaped scar on my chest to prove it. I was brought back alive twice when everyone thought I wouldn't last a week.

Porencephalic cyst. An extremely rare disorder of the central nervous system involving a cyst or cavity inside the brain tissue. I had a hole in my brain.

Hemiparesis is a weakness on one side of the body. The patient can move the impaired side of his body but with reduced muscular strength. This is obvious; you can see it.

Bowel obstruction** born, unable to make bowel movements. (I couldn't poop when I was born)

Hypotonia: reduced muscle strength.

It all boiled down to cerebral palsy, which wasn't diagnosed for a year.

I was born at 2lbs 2oz. My dad could lift me with one hand as Raffiki does to Simba. My entire hand was the size of his thumb.

With all that craziness, my parents never knew if I would live or die, and I cost them a quarter million dollars in hospital bills. I spent three months in that hospital going through all sorts of random procedures and surgeries to stay alive. But I did it. I lived. God sure had a plan for me, though I'm still discovering daily what His plan is.

All in all, my childhood was great. I guess we all say that, though.

I've always struggled with physical activity. Before I could walk, I was seen shuffling around on my knees. My kneecaps were as thick and calloused as a Hobbit's feet. Once my legs were strong enough, I used a walker to get around. According to my parents, I had the spirit of a highly active young boy in those early years, even if I lacked the ability of one.

I was always very upfront about my disability with new people. I still am. I would begin each school year in elementary school with a presentation in front of the class. I would stand there with my Physical Therapist and explain: "Hi, my name is Sam. I have something called cerebral palsy. It means that my left arm and leg don't work well. I'm like everyone else, except I need help with scissors and carrying heavy stuff, and you won't see me run on the playground. Thanks!"

The friends I made were gracious. They never treated me any differently from anyone else in the group. Games of baseball, tag, or wall-ball, were easily adapted to accommodate my limited ability.

When they would race ahead on bicycles (to this day, I cannot ride one), I would turn to books. I thought nothing of it. Things were simple back then. Things only grew more complicated as my body grew more twisted.

My mother reacted the way any mother would have responded, given her situation. She protected me. Granted, her idea of protection manifested itself as a subconscious "Sam can't (fill in the blank: tie his shoes, cut his food, button his shirts, etc.) by himself, I need to help." The typical overprotective mother reached a level never before seen. I was not bothered to cut my steak until I was sixteen; mom always did it for me. To this day, I have never ordered a steak dinner on a first date. Everyone has something to hide, something that isn't first-date material. My dark secret is that I make a mess cutting meat. Sorry ladies, but you have to earn that level of trust.

Ah, Middle School. That awkward time between child and teenager (reword). Hormones are developing, identities are taking shape, and grades are starting to matter. Honestly, middle school was some of my best years (reword). The schoolwork was challenging enough that I felt proud to get A's, my friendships grew deeper than ever, and I got a true taste of the limelight in drama class (which would later develop into a lifelong devotion to theater). Little did I know that my identity would be reborn in these critical years, not unlike the rebirth of the legendary phoenix.

The Nickname Day

Forgive me if I ramble during this next bit; there is quite a lot to say. I guess I'll start with Nickname Day. I remember it perfectly. Sitting in the back of Homeroom during a break, the football team quarterback was giving out nicknames to his friends. I piped up, not to be left out (pun always intended).

"Hey man, what's my nickname?" I was met with an awkward silence. Joey squirmed in his seat.

"I, uh . . . I can only think of one, but I don't wanna say it," he whispered nervously. I chuckled. Surely a nickname can't be all bad. I challenged him to spit it out. He fumbled a little and then choked out "Uh . . . cripple." I laughed and nodded at the coolest kid in sixth grade. I thought nothing of it. I was just glad to be accepted by the cool crowd finally. From then on and to this day, I was known as Cripple. Later this nickname would be adapted to CC or Christian Cripple.

I look back now and marvel. It is only recently that I learned that the word "cripple" creates tension within the disabled community (I am much newer to all of this than my hotheaded counterpart). Back then, it was just a name. My friends used Cripple as a term of endearment. Granted, it was abused by people who were not friends — more on that later.

Several people in my life do not understand why I choose to take ownership of a slander like "cripple." My brother nearly beat up a friend who yelled, "Hey, cripple!" in greeting. I don't hold it against those who think I am degrading myself by openly calling myself a cripple. The way I see it, I am accepting a part of who I am. Does this mean that my disability or my limitations define me? By no means. I constantly push my boundaries, and any athlete would tell you it is the only way to improve.

P90x and other manly things

It was in seventh grade that my true strength was revealed. Until then, my friends saw me as physically weak (to the casual observer, it would be a logical assumption), and I was happy to uphold the facade.

But one day, I was pushed too far. In the locker room before P.E., we joked as adolescent boys do.

My friend made a snide comment about my inability to run with the rest of the group, and I lashed out. Faster than anyone thought possible, I swung my right arm at the accuser. I landed a perfect punch on his arm, right below his shoulder, and was rewarded with a cry of pain!

"OWWW! What the fuck . . . that's not supposed to hurt! You're the Cripple! You can't hurt me!" It turns out I delivered an instantaneous dead arm. I laughed and explained, "Think about it. I've used my right arm for everything these last twelve years of my life when you use both arms. I have cripple strength!" This was met with a resounding laugh, and I spent the next ten minutes punching my friends in the arms as hard as I could. I like to think that was a turning point in my life. For the first time in my life, I felt *strong*.

Identity

Who are you?

You control your destiny.

You can do anything you set your mind to.

These questions and motivational phrases barrage us daily. I have a serious problem with the last one. Let's face it. There are plenty of things that I will never be able to do. I can never be a gymnast. I will never be able to win a bodybuilding competition. I may never be able to run a marathon. But guess what? That's okay.

It is perfectly fine to look at your life and evaluate what you can accomplish and disregard the rest. We have to be okay with this.

I am not saying that we should never push ourselves to pursue bigger and better dreams. I am not saying that in the slightest. What I am trying to say is, let's be realistic about the dreams we work towards. Not everyone is going to grow up to be President. That's okay.

When I was a child, my aspirations changed, like everyone's did at a young age. The day I got my first tricycle, I wanted to be a taxi driver. I spent hours pedaling around our circular driveway, screaming how mustard would make me strong. A few short years after that, I wanted to be an actor (live, on stage). That dream was dismissed and squashed by my well-intentioned older brother, who reasoned that I would be typecast as a "crippled actor." From that day on, my affinity for the limelight was pushed to the back burner and eventually faded to a fleeting hobby.

I was never really upset at my brother for this. I am glad that he made me look realistically at my dream. Looking back, I would not be happy learning to dance and sing my way across a stage. It's just not in me to do so. I still greatly enjoy the odd game of improv with friends, but I have found a new passion: literature, and as of this writing, I am a certified librarian. One "failed" dream gave birth to a fulfilling and joyous career. That's okay.

Another aspect of this theme, "you can do anything," is the pressure of pleasing those around you. We must be careful with this. We can get so caught up in wanting to make (fill in the blank: dad, mom, grandparents, aunt, uncle, God) proud that we often ignore what makes us *happy.* Too often, I have seen people waste time, energy, and resources pursuing certain things in life only to reach a moment when they look back and say, "I did all of this to make you proud, and now it's my turn to live."

Why don't we cut out the middleman and live for ourselves first? It comes down to two people and two people only: You and God. When pursuing happiness (and, in this evolving context, a career), one should only truly be concerned with where God leads.

CHAPTER 21

SAM I AM II

By: Samuel Maupin

Washington, USA

Introduction

My name is Sam Maupin, independent journalist, broadcaster, shock Comedian, mixed martial artist, Christian, dirt biker, Loud mouth and a few more. To describe myself, I am an athletic independent person. You will know me by my strange walk (which helps in bad parts of town), my shit-eating grin and my slightly slimy good manners. But to kick this off, I guess I should start at the beginning, that wonderful time when we fool ourselves into thinking we were ignorant and sheltered. This might be true of me, or might not, that's for you to decide.

Childhood

There is a lot of my childhood I don't remember, but what I do remember was a loving family, woods, trees and an imagination that never stopped. When I was young I was a little obsessed with the ocean and the stars. From baby beluga, to Sea-quest, to Star Trek, I was completely and totally in love with science fiction. The movie "Twenty Thousand Leagues Under the Sea" was my favorite. I saw myself as a special person, but not a limited person. I knew deep down that I was going to conquer the stars and dive to the bottom of the sea.

My parents made no attempt to ever stop these dreams. In fact looking back, they are still the most all-embracing people I have ever met. Now, the CP made for an interesting childhood. My first assumptions were that it was not a disability, but proof that I was from another world. As a child, I imagined that the CP was my true form and my body was nothing but a bad disguise — a bad disguise I needed to take off. Whatever other people thought, my parents never tried to argue with my own fantastic version of reality. Some childhood friends did try to convince me otherwise, some of whom may be reading this now. To them I say, I wish we could go back to that time. My parents still have a self-portrait I drew of a spiky looking alien figure.

In the beginning I was totally accepting and completely oblivious to teasing or people mocking me. Although there was an incident I vaguely remember. I remember coming back from a playground, my mother was angry, and said "If those kids ever do that again I will shake them up and throw them." It took years for the memory to surface.

Later on in my last year of community college, while I was in an interpersonal communications class, reading through a textbook section on Social Isolation, my older sister told me what had happened. Little tiny me had been noticed by a group of other children. Whether they were bigger, older, or whatever, they noticed the braces on my feet and something happened. I'm guessing they made fun of the braces, or the different walk, or something like that. Whatever it was, I was found, shirtless, laying face up on the dirt surrounded by blank stares. My sister said I was totally and completely alone, and it took weeks for little me to come forward and say what had happened. This event and others like it would turn a child into a teenager, and later a man, with zero humanity.

I became an unstoppable competitive force with anger as hot as the sun, and I'm still burning.

As I grew older, teasing started to make more sense, and I felt the sting of social rejection. I became shy of new people and afraid of my peers. My parents still took me and my little brother hiking, biking and I still spent time with friends. I loved to climb trees. Every time I climbed I felt truly free. I did fall now and then and a few times my best friend and I did run out of daylight and got stuck. If you're wondering, I still do climb trees. On occasion my fifteen-year-old nephew and I will pull ourselves into the branches of an old evergreen and climb until we break through the canopy.

One part of my childhood that was important but always understated, were my religious views. My mother would always read bible stories. I prayed regularly, there was never a question in my mind to the existence of God. At the bad times I prayed, and cried, but never doubted the existence of God. God kept me from falling out of the trees, and even if I did slip, it was god that kept me from dying.

Heaven was the place where my neighbor who had the heart attack went, along with my grandfather (On my dad's side) and my family's many pets, (dogs, cats, birds, hamsters, rats and dead mice the cats brought) though I've run out of black ink to count the sins, and times I've missed the mark, that knowledge of god has never left.

If I had any advice to my younger self it would be… not all people are assholes, but still be sure to watch your back, never stop competing, trust me you'll get upstaged and shamed, but that's all the more reason to keep going.

I'm not going to say don't give up on your dreams, let's face it, things like dating people twenty years older than you when you're nine isn't realistic, and very few people actually go to the stars, but don't be afraid to pick up new dreams and try new things.

To the parents of children like I was, I hate to say it . . . but I'm afraid your child will have an interesting life. If they come to you for help, please be a parent, but whatever you do, do not take that away from them. Let them have an adventure, and don't rain on their parades when they try to compete, and don't try to ever hold them back from trying something new . . .

Ok, maybe not meth or Heroin, or jumping off cliffs (use some common sense) but don't baby them, because you can't control what future is going to throw at them, and that thing they did once and loved might save their lives in the future.

Last but not least, to the bullies, whether you're on the playground, in the classroom or church. I can't speak to your situation, but I can say this, trust me… don't do it. Without diving away, I didn't stay small forever, or weak. The little kid you may pick on today will come years later burning with hate.

Don't believe me? Look at history, I guarantee every terrible mass murderer and dictator wasn't born that way, hate is something you get somewhere, and you're basically bringing hell on the future, so be nice… Or for the sake of everyone around you, try to spread love not hate… it does matter.

Self-Identify
This is the first piece of biographical writing I have ever done, but it must be written, or at least attempted. Listen to the YouTube link for some context

https://www.youtube.com/watch?v=kHub8SQmngk

First off, a word of encouragement I can give. Let each mile you walk, push-up you do, or page you write, be a declaration of independence. Don't think of yourself as an inspiration, think of yourself as a freedom fighter on the front lines, every time you shine, ground is gained.

Through my life as a person with a disability and a person with CP, the struggle with anger and hate is a real one and even as an adult, it's still the biggest challenge I face. If I could share a coffee with God, I'd ask him, why have you given me so much hate? Why do I feel so much rage? What is the reason for this fire inside me that will never stop?

Without going into too much detail, I will say this; even with the passing of the ADA, discrimination is real and we've all had to face it in one form or another. For me, it was always the speed at which I work. I am a broadcaster by trade. If I had a penny for the amount of times I've heard the words, "You don't work fast enough," I could pay the college tuition of three people.

For me, aside from disability, the temptation to cast aside due process and civility and be violent, to trade the protest sign for the gun is real. As a teenager I started working out, after a couple years of tai kwan do, toughen up my knuckles, and punch. I remember putting those knuckles to use a few times and they give me a feeling of power. I graduated from Kyokushin Karate my second year of college and found that CP actually was a god given gift in sparring. I could hit harder, and take hits all day . . . on the CP side.

While building my body boosted myself esteem, I realized that in truth I was capable of killing and maiming using the same thing that was labeled a "disability" and slowly myself identity shifted, from a person with a disability.

The idea of others breaking out of this label like I have lurks in the back of my head like a ghost. After hearing words like "Sorry, but you're not fast enough", enough times, the question remains, do we try to fit in, or do we risk our lives in the hopes of someday never needing to "fit in again." Would the disabled community even consider coming together under the banner of militancy?

Based on my time in the community, I feel confident that each individual would find their place. Whether it was hacking websites, recruiting, designing assistive technology for fighting or guerilla warfare, we would all fit together like gears in a machine. I've played with the sci-fi idea of a disabled army so much it's almost become boring to me. But would we even want to fight back?

Over my years in college, I always bounded better with other minorities, the common thread was always there, thus, my struggle. But one piece of encouragement I can give. Let each mile you walk, push up you do, or page you write be a declaration of independence.

CHAPTER 22

HOW TO TURN IMPOSSIBLE INTO I'M POSSIBLE

By: Tabetha Burley

Ontario, Canada

www.rollingwithme.com

What would happen to you if tomorrow you woke up and were in a wheelchair? Would you feel sorry for yourself? Would you succumb to the challenge and live the rest of your days never going places or doing anything again? Or would you see the challenge, raise the bar and push forward to live your best life?

I, Tabetha Judith Marie Burley, have, without a doubt, chosen to live a very active, fun and fulfilling life thus far and do not plan on changing that anytime soon. I was born two months premature, weighing only 2 lbs. 2 oz, and at nine months, I was diagnosed with spastic quadriplegia cerebral palsy (CP). In my case, I do not have any torso balance which means I cannot walk or stand independently, and it also affects the hyper tone, which means there is stiffness in both my arms and legs.

Many surgeries also occurred, including an operation to uncross my eyes and two operations to help reduce the spasticity in my legs and feet to assist with movement. My parents were told I would never walk, talk, read, write or do anything for myself independently and I would need assistance getting in and out of things.

I proved all the doctors wrong! Just goes to show with perseverance and determination, almost anything is possible.

In school and elsewhere, I have never had any trouble making friends and have never been bullied. I want the next generation of people with challenges coming along to know that even though the world is very different now from when I was growing up with the Internet and bullying, know that your differences can and will become your strengths and if you are open to situations and experiences being adapted, you too can conquer anything.

One of the most essential components to being able to do this effectively is always being honest about your challenge, whether visible or not. Being open and willing to talk to people about it. Children are not afraid to approach and ask questions; it's the adults who always pull them away from the situation. As a result of being open to the conversation, this will help to change the way society has been unconsciously conditioned to shy away from or even avoid to the point of not including people with differences. Forget what the textbooks say and show everyone practical and innovative solutions.

Two specific people that have been very influential in my path and purpose to who I have become today are my Granddad and Rick Hansen. In 1987 Rick was on his "Man in Motion" World tour, where he pushed himself around the world in a manual wheelchair. Accompanying each tour stop, Rick had chosen people to meet and greet him, and at seven years old, I was selected to represent him at one of the stops he made throughout Southwestern Ontario. While Rick proved that pushing himself around the world in a manual wheelchair was possible, it inspired me, as a wheelchair user, that anything is possible.

My granddad was a minister and was always kind and willing to help people, wanting nothing in return.

I know I was also given this gift through him, where I have an innate ability to sense and can feel what people are experiencing. Therefore, I find it very easy to connect with people and ask the right questions to expand people's thinking when they feel stuck or need someone to support them through hard times. I have been told countless times that I have an innate ability to know when to lift people's spirits or moods whenever needed, maybe without even knowing it, but little do they know I already know exactly what is required. I have never been afraid to speak up for myself or someone who cannot do so for themselves. I am always there to help anyone I can if they are open to it, and best of all, they have a trustworthy friend in me as a result.

I was raised, supported and encouraged to be included in anything in my school years and beyond. My peers and anyone involved in my life have never seen the wheelchair first or as a roadblock, but Tabetha, as a person first, who happens to use a wheelchair as a primary means of mobility and independence. I have never felt I missed out on anything in my life because I always involve myself in all things to the best of MY ABILITY; though I am not able-bodied, I am still very able.

I am very adventurous and love anything fast, and I am competitive. I have been active in sports like swimming, downhill sit-skiing, hand-cycling, water skiing, snowmobiling and atv'ing. If it was not for being open to water skiing, hand cycling and sit-skiing being adapted, it would be the difference between being able to have the experience or not. So, there was no time to think about not doing it.

Aside from adaptive sports, I have also succeeded academically and professionally. I have been a licensed real estate broker for the last six years.

Before this career change, though finding a place of employment that is also accessible and having transportation can be a roadblock sometimes, in my mind, there is always a way to work around it. I elected to do my post-secondary education online, receiving a diploma in information technology, allowing me to do websites for individuals and companies. Once this became too competitive, I needed to find a new career path. I then began the journey of my two passions wanting to help people and advocating for accessibility for people with physical, developmental and visual challenges. I started by joining the municipal accessibility committee, running for a municipal councillor in 2014, 2018 and 2022 elections and attending/speaking at council meetings. In 2015 the Accessibility Ontario Disability Act (AODA) Presented me with the tenth anniversary champion award for being a leader in my community for accessibility and inclusion.

Wouldn't it be refreshing if people chose to see ability versus inability? If they did not assume a person with challenges is forever dependent on someone? To lessen the ignorance, human rights and Accessibility Ontario Disability Act (AODA) training should be mandatory and implemented in all on-the-job training. Another observation I have made for years is the accessibility and "equal opportunity" that are included in guidelines and policies for hiring purposes, without the follow-through of accessibility throughout buildings, including entries, washrooms and a means of transportation to get to and from the job, it makes it very frustrating and most times not feasible to obtain a job even if we are qualified to hold the position.

Part of the ignorance is not being educated or understanding all the needs and being taught when something or someone is "different" not to ask questions for fear of offending.

How will society ever evolve and break the pattern if this behaviour continues to be acceptable? It is not possible, and change needs to happen now!!

Since getting into real estate, one of my missions is to find and work with a developer(s) and/or an investor(s) who will see and share my vision to make all homes, commercial and public spaces barrier-free and accessible to all.

An additional area that needs to be addressed is people requiring any mobility device, modifications to homes or adapted accessible vehicles. We need to make all of these more affordable to obtain versus having the people feel like they have to remain restricted simply because they are too expensive to obtain because we are a minority population. If we cannot work for legitimate reasons or transportation versus choosing not to work. In these cases, we need our governments to acknowledge that we currently have to live below the poverty line.

If on assistance due to these funds being used for rent and then our needs for care, transportation and mobility devices, this, in turn, leaves little to no extra money for food and clothing, let alone something extra to enjoy. This, too, has to change to reflect the cost of living in all areas today. We are not put in these circumstances by choice; these are a need, not a want based on prestige ranking. They are needed to ensure we can live our lives with quality and in the most fulfilled and independent way possible.

I am known to be a very open-minded, positive, confident, tenacious and vibrant individual with a smile that lights up a room and always gets noticed. I encourage everyone in my immediate circle and beyond to be positive and forward-thinking.

People often ask me how I remain so happy, driven and motivated.

Everything is a matter of perspective. Able-bodied people always view my inability to walk independently and roll versus walk as an unfortunate limitation. However, for me, it is not like I once knew what it was like to walk or that I lost that ability due to a tragic event. For me having all the abilities that able-bodied people view as "normal," whatever that means anyway. I have nothing to compare to, so anything I cannot do in the usual way is not a loss from my point of view because I always find a way to do it and/or be part of the experience.

Everything in life is an experience, and what you choose to make it, and what you choose to do with it will determine the outcome and where you end up. It is a lifelong journey that sometimes needs help from someone who lives with daily challenges, someone who can show that having limitations does not mean a lack of motivation or achievement. The challenges can be considered an asset as we are forced to think ahead, think differently than the general population, and accept that not everyone can or will understand the struggles to gain true perspective. Believe it or not, people with any challenge, be it visible or not, we still have goals, dreams and aspirations just like everyone else.

To change the way society has been conditioned to believe that if anyone or anything is different than the prescribed definition of "normal" or a path you must follow, the idea or passion is not worth pursuing. People need to hear and see there are always ways to make anything go from a dream to reality, no matter what the circumstances or limiting beliefs are in your mind.

Our whole world has so much untapped potential due to the limits we believe and, as a result, have to be placed on everything . . . just think, how powerful is that? So, what or who is stopping you from reaching your full potential to pursue your passion and live your best life? YOU!! I would love to be the mentor and motivational speaker to spearhead this much-needed and long-overdue change FINALLY!

You may have noticed throughout my chapter, I have NEVER used the words "disability" or "disabled." I have always felt that these words already have people starting with a negative thought, as the word "dis" has a "not able" or "negative" meaning associated with it. I hope I have shown you throughout my journey that I and many others in similar situations are capable; it just may be in an adapted way and, more importantly, a change of your mindset to make anything happen.

If any part of my journey has resonated with you, from being a very resourceful problem solver, having the ability to feel and sense what people are experiencing, to my passion for advocacy with accessibility in real estate and beyond, and you want/need help with your journey, please feel free to reach out to me. I am here and can work with YOU to come up with achievable steps to break through whatever your barriers are, and if you are willing to change your mindset, it always turns the IMPOSSIBLE to I'M POSSIBLE!

CHAPTER 23

THE SKY'S THE LIMIT

By: Tammy McLeod, PLY

Ontario, Canada

In the early morning of February 15th, 1977, my mother started to bleed. She called her family doctor in Parkhill, and he told her to go to St. Joseph's Hospital as soon as possible. At the time, my parents lived in Strathroy, Ontario, so they had to drive about forty minutes to get there. When they got to the hospital, my mother was hemorrhaging pretty badly. The nurses and doctor had to prepare her for an unexpected C-section in order to get me out quickly. It was a tense and serious situation for my young parents. My father told the doctor to please save us both. What happened was my mother was hemorrhaging, and the placenta came before I did; therefore, I was being suffocated and was losing oxygen to my brain. Thankfully, they were able to get me out by C-section and save both my mother and me.

My parents noticed that I wasn't doing some of the things that babies normally do, so they consulted a doctor about it. At fifteen months old, I was diagnosed with Spastic Quad Cerebral Palsy. Spastic Quad CP is when all four limbs are affected, where muscles are stiff and tight and have involuntary movement.

This is caused by damage to the Motor Cortex. The motor cortex is located in the cerebral cortex, which is the largest part of the brain.

The motor cortex is composed of several parts that are responsible for relaying signals to other parts of the brain to control movement. In my case, lack of oxygen to the brain during birth caused the damage. This has affected my ability to walk without assistance, and I have a speech impairment.

Funny facts about having CP are the CP shivers, which are an involuntary movement of the body and the reflex of jumping at things. My family and friends love this fact. They try to scare me for fun just to see me jump out of my skin. I remember one time while living with my best friend, she came home from work, and I was sitting out on the balcony reading a book. The balcony door was closed; and I didn't hear her come home. She went to the door, and BANG! I probably jumped five feet in the air. She almost pissed herself from laughing.

When I was two years old, the doctors advised my parents that it would be best for me to go live at CPRI (Child and Parent Resource Institute) in London, Ontario, for treatment. Since this was all new for my parents, they went along with the advice of the doctors. My family would come on the weekends to visit me, and when they went to leave, they could hear me screaming for them from a window. I was there until my parents said this was enough . . . we are taking our baby home. I still went there for treatment, I just didn't live there. I don't remember my time there, and my mom says that it may be a good thing that I don't. However, they were the ones who potty trained me and taught me how to communicate with the bliss board.

The doctors told my parents that I would never walk, talk, ride a bike, or do a lot of things. This wasn't in the cards for me. Right from the get-go, I have had the determination and fight in me to climb any obstacles or barriers that I face in life.

I grew up much like any other kid in the small town of Strathroy. When I was three years old, I started going to nursery school in a local church with able-bodied kids. It was a way for me to interact with other kids and be included in normal things. When I was four years old, I went to Thames Valley Children's Centre in London. Every day, I was bussed there from Strathroy. It was like preschool, in a way. I was in a class with other disabled kids. The teachers taught us things like how to write and tie our shoes; we went swimming, we played outside on the playground, we watched kid's TV shows, etc. I loved it there.

In addition to me, I also have a brother who is a year younger than me. We are typical siblings and would fight over the stupidest things growing up. He liked to pull my pigtails when he got mad at me. Growing up, I would talk on the phone with my friends for hours. I think that is why I got my own phone line . . . my parents were getting tired of never being able to use the phone. As you can see, I was a normal kid doing what any able-bodied kid would do. It was just a matter of finding alternative ways to accomplish some things since sometimes they were more challenging. There were a lot of challenges and barriers that came along with most of the things that I wanted to do. However, I would never give up or say no; I can't do this; I found a way to fight through them and found the self-confidence that I needed to do them. One of the things that helped me with this was going to Woodeden Easter Seals Camp every summer for fourteen years, plus respite once a month when I was a teen. I loved camp! It was my home away from home. It was a chance for me to get away from everyday life and all the barriers and just have fun.

It helped with my self-confidence and taught me how I could be more independent.

This was a place where I didn't have to worry about being treated differently or anyone feeling sorry for me. I truly miss it to this day!

I started to attend regular school after TVCC. I went to the same public school from kindergarten to grade eight in Strathroy. When I started grade one, I was given an EA to help me in the classroom with writing notes and anything I needed help with. I had the same person all through to grade ten; then, I got a new EA for my last two years of high school. I was lucky to have the same person for all those years!

One thing that I did differently than other kids, though, is that I had to attend Thames Valley Children's Centre in London for physiotherapy and speech therapy.

Sometimes a physiotherapist came to my public school to do my therapy so that I didn't miss a lot of school. Without TVCC, I probably wouldn't be walking or talking the way that I am today. I also have had a few surgeries in my life. I had my legs operated on to cut the tendons to loosen them to help me walk better. I had my saliva glands removed to help me not drool, I had my eyes operated on to try to improve my lazy eye (I am blind in my left eye), and I had several dental surgeries.

When it was time for high school, it was a difficult time for me. Unfortunately, the high school in my hometown at that time wasn't wheelchair accessible. Therefore, I had to go elsewhere. My parents gave me two choices — either Parkhill or Glencoe. I didn't want either of them because I wanted to go with my friends. But unfortunately, I had to make that hard choice. I went with Parkhill. It was tough because I didn't know anybody, and I was the only person in a wheelchair there.

My first year was hard, and I remember coming home crying because I wasn't happy not being with my friends. The school and my parents found a way to help me adjust better.

A couple of times, I was allowed to bring a friend to school with me. It helped me adjust better and fit in more smoothly. I even went to school in Strathroy with my friends for a day. My guys' friends helped me get around by carrying me up and down the stairs. It was a fun day! I started making friends in grade ten, which got better for me. I was doing all the things that teenagers were doing. The only thing that I needed to adapt to was not being allowed to participate in any gym classes in high school. The school felt that it was too unsafe for me. They, however, let me practice my boccia in a hallway during my spare time and let anyone play with me if they didn't have a class.

After high school, I decided to go to college. At the age of nineteen, I moved out from my parent's house to my own apartment in London, Ontario, to attend Fanshawe College in the Office Administration course. I had a roommate but had to kick her out after four months. Although I liked being in London close to my friends and family, I decided that I needed to make a bigger move. After one year in London, I decided to attend Cambrian College in Sudbury, Ontario, to take more business courses. I lived in residence for the two years that I was there. There were some challenges that I had to face, but with my determination and my never-give-up attitude, I found a way to overcome them. I had Home Care come in every day to assist me with my personal care needs two times a day. I moved back to London in 1999 after finishing school. However, going to Sudbury was the best move that I made because I learned how to be even more independent and how not to rely on people so much for things.

In 2001, I was accepted into the Direct Funding Program. It is a provincial program for people with disabilities to hire their own personal support workers. I have workers come in every day to assist me with my daily needs.

This has changed my life for the better! I can live a normal life without the burden of having to deal with a healthcare agency.

From 2006-2013, I lived in an apartment with my best friend. After 2013, I had my own apartment again, until 2019, I had to make the decision to move back with my parents as rent prices were outrageous. I was trying to get a mortgage to buy my own place, but I kept getting denied because I am an Ontario Disability Support Program recipient, and they don't look at anything else. Not giving up, though. I will be on my own again!

I have been involved in sports pretty much my whole life. I first started bowling in the Youth Bowling League at the age of six. It was a chance for me to do a sport along with my peers/friends. However, I couldn't stand and throw a ball down the alley, so my dad had to build me a ramp to use. I sat on a normal chair with my ramp on my lap to propel the ball down. I got good at it and was beginning to compete in tournaments until the Youth Bowling Council told me that I couldn't compete because they felt like I was at an advantage by using a ramp. I was eight years old at this time. My parents and I thought that it wasn't right of them to tell me that I couldn't participate, that it was unfair, and that I was being discriminated against.

My parents asked me, "What do you want to do?"

I said, "I want to fight."

We took the YBC to court and won. Nevertheless, there was a long delay as they appealed the decision for eight years, but I didn't give up on it.

By the end of it, I wasn't bowling anymore, but I was doing it more for other disabled kids rather than myself. I wanted other disabled kids to have the right to compete in bowling if they choose to.

My case was well-known across Canada. It even got into Universities' textbooks. To this day, it is still online and in books. Also, ramps have been placed in most bowling alleys all over.

I then started swimming competitively. I was on a swim team named the London Lightning Bolts. It was for disabled kids/teens. We held our practices at the YMCA in downtown London. I only competed provincially because the classification that I was in was a very low class for people who had to wear a swimming device, and it wasn't included in most competitions. But my dream since childhood was to represent Canada at the Paralympic Games. One day, my teammate and her parents told me about boccia and that they knew someone who was involved with it. They said that they thought that it may be something that I might like and that I should check it out. The person that they knew was Debbie Willows, who is a two-time Paralympian, and who founded a local tournament called Boccia Blast. It was October 1991, and my parents and I went to the tournament to meet Debbie and check boccia out. Debbie let me try it, and that was it...I was hooked! In the beginning, I competed in both swimming and boccia, but it got to be too much for me. I had to make a decision on what I wanted to do. I knew somehow that boccia was going to take me places, so I chose it. Boy, was I ever right! I competed in boccia for twenty-seven years. Not only did I qualify to represent Canada at the Paralympic Games once, but four times! The Paralympic Games that I have competed in are 2000 in Sydney, Australia; 2004 in Athens, Greece; 2008 in Beijing, China; and 2012 in London, England.

171

In 2015, I had the honour of representing Canada at the ParaPan Am Games held in Toronto. My Team and I won the bronze medal in the Team Event.

It was an incredible experience, especially being on home soil! Throughout my career, I have won several awards, including the 2000 & 2007 Athlete of the Year, and I was a Finalist for the 2007 Ontario Female with a Disability of the Year award. I also received the Queen Elizabeth II Diamond Jubilee Medal for my participation in the 2012 Paralympic Games.

In September 2018, I retired from being a Boccia athlete. It was a bittersweet moment for me when I announced my retirement. I was going to wait until the end of the year, but it seemed like it was the right time. I was ready to turn the page from this exciting chapter of my life and embark on the next new chapter. I haven't gotten out of the boccia world completely. After retirement, I Co-Founded a little boccia business with an old teammate called All In One Boccia Services, but due to COVID, business slowed way down. I am now a Certified Coach. I love coaching and watching the athletes improve. I am the Vice-President of the London Cannonballs Boccia Club. We host an annual boccia tournament called Boccia Blast, and I am the Co-Chair on the Hosting Committee.

Being involved in sports has been huge for me. It has given me the tools to succeed in life and the mental skills to deal with situations in life. It has opened doors to things that otherwise might not have happened. However, with sports, I also made some low points, especially when I developed my injuries. Most of my injuries were caused by overuse. I had to maintain the pain and flexibility by doing a lot of stretching and physio along with laser therapy.

Having these injuries on top of my CP is hard because my muscles are always sore and tight, to begin with. Even though I'm not playing anymore, I still have to do a lot of stretching and laser therapy, and I try to do physio.

I experience a lot of muscle spasms and pain in my everyday life.

I also have done some exciting things in my life. I went water skiing and water tubing, which was so much fun! I have even been parasailing three times, once in BC, once in Australia, and once in Punta Cana. The whole experience was breathtaking! I even had the chance to go on the Great Wall of China, thanks to my coach, who carried me on his back all the way up! I was able to check off one other thing that I had on my bucket list.

While at the 2015 ParaPan Am Games in Toronto, I went ziplining on the waterfront with my mom and two friends. Although it was just a little line, it was an amazing feeling to finally be able to do it. Also, summer of 2017, I was able to raise that by going on the zipline in Niagara Falls. It was so awesome! I have attended so many concerts that I lost count. I will admit, it is nice having a disability when I go to concerts as sometimes it helps me get in first and get special treatment…hee hee. I have been on four cruises, which I loved. I have participated in a 5km walk/run on the Jillian Michaels cruise, which I managed to walk 4km of! I did it by pushing my manual chair. When I told my friends and mom that I wanted to do it, they thought it would be a crazy thing for me to do. However, they knew that once I set my mind to do something, I was going to do it — so they all joined me!

It was an amazing feeling knowing that I was accomplishing something that I'd always wanted to try to do! But boy, did I ever pay for it that night and the next day.

I was in so much leg pain that I couldn't bear weight, and I was up most of the night in tears. However, if you ask me if I would do it again, my answer would be yes in a heartbeat!

People are always telling me that I am a role model and/or an inspiration, but I don't see myself as that. I am just living my life. I am lucky to have family and friends who never treat me any differently than everyone else.

Yes, living with a disability is hard, but I always keep going. I don't let my CP define who I am. I just need to approach most things from a different angle. This, however, doesn't mean I don't have the same needs and wants as able-bodied people.

I never give up on anything. I always tell people to embrace life, don't take anything for granted and keep their dreams alive! I am a CP WARRIOR!

Epilogue

The purpose of this collaboration book is for each of us to share our personal stories about living with cerebral palsy. Challenges that could easily have stopped us from pursuing our dreams and aspirations. We have chosen to move forward and create our dreams that are important to us. Our strength and determination is what continues to motivate us, and to reach our personal goals. We expect respect and dignity as well as inclusion.

It is our hope that our stories will inspire and strengthen you, and that they will inspire the next generation of people living with CP to *NEVER* give up, to *FIGHT* for what they want, to never take anything for *GRANTED*, and just to *EMBRACE* life because life is what *YOU* make it!

On behalf of my global friends, and I would like to express our gratitude for purchasing a copy of this book and taking the time to read our stories.

Please spread this book to your family and friends!

If you enjoyed this book, we would love a review on Amazon.

About the Book Creator

Kyle is Canadian-born, given a life against all odds when diagnosed with a physical disability called Cerebral Palsy at sixteen months. However, all the love and support from his village have made him a stronger person.

Kyle always has determination, and a never-give-up attitude, can show compassion, is patient with others, and sees the good in people even when they may not see it in themselves.

Cerebral Palsy changed Kyle's life in many ways, but he ultimately controls his life. Kyle has the steering wheel and always does his best to navigate the road ahead.

While Kyle graduated college as an architectural technician, he still struggles to integrate into a world that is ill-equipped for those with disabilities. While struggling to find his purpose in the architectural field, he wrote a memoir about his life with Cerebral Palsy without knowing that his career as an author would exceed all his expectations. As a result of his memoir reaching the bestseller lists, he has significantly impacted the lives of others, encouraging them to be the best they can be and follow their dreams.

Manufactured by Amazon.ca
Bolton, ON

33158832R00104